SMALL IN THE EYE OF A RIVER

FRANK MELE

SMALL
IN THE EYE
OF A RIVER

❊

FRANK MELE

THE LYONS PRESS

To my son and daughter,
Andre and Angela,
riches beyond reward

ISBN 1-55821-963-3

CONTENTS

INTRODUCTION
- vii -

BLUE DUN
-1-

A FISHING TALE
-23-

THE MASTERS
-33-

A PHOENIX FOR DAN
-46-

ONCE IN A BLUE DUN MOON
-54-

SAINT THEODORE'S JACKET
-68-

THOUGHTS ON FLY FISHING
-77-

FAREWELL TO FLY FISHING
-110-

THE MAYFLIES
-130-

ENVOI
-148-

BIOGRAPHY
-149-

INTRODUCTION

THE ELUSIVE COLOR of a fine blue dun cape comes closest to defining the quality of a Frank Mele essay or tale on fly fishing. There is change and surprise. There is the sure sense that we are not touching something merely material, but a thing of this world that holds mystery—and perhaps, in its exquisite specialness, something absolutely not duplicatable, carrying a rare delicacy and a rare capacity to touch the heart.

I was proud to have published Frank's "Blue Dun" in *Fisherman's Bounty,* an anthology I compiled nearly thirty years ago. It was, I think, the most unusual and original selection in that book. Since then I have been asked dozens of times, "Who is Frank Mele?"—for this was his only published essay on fly fishing and he was to write only a few more pieces in the following years—each different, each trying to capture and define, either head-on or through the agency of the tale, the parable, some special aspect of the world of the fly fisher.

As a professional musician, Frank has had an extensive career in symphony and chamber music as violinist with the Rochester Philharmonic and later, violist with the Pittsburgh Symphony and the Modern Art String Quartet. For many years he has taught both instruments privately and composed works for stringed instruments for young people. Music has been so much a part of Frank's life that it informs and lives in every word he has written.

Steadily, over the years, Frank had been building an impressive body of prose. His novel *Polpetto* was published by Crown Publishers in the early 1970s and received high praise; his remarkable story "The Inheritance," which has been anthologized, has been called "a minor masterpiece."

Fly fishing, like music and fine prose, comes from the deepest part of Frank. Essentially a private man, his great love of rivers led him to found the small but potent group, *Catskill Waters,* which waged a long and fierce campaign to save the Catskill rivers from the depredations of New York City. It achieved a landmark victory which was translated into law. He ties flies sparingly, exquisitely; he fly fishes with immense care; he collects blue dun necks and bamboo and is forever searching for the ultimate shade and texture, the ultimate rod that will meet all his exacting dry-fly demands, under varying conditions.

The same restless, searching quality characterizes his essays and tales on fly fishing. He has brought an absolutely new voice to angling literature—delicate, elusive, speculative, searching, earthy, witty, and ultimately wise.

I envy those of you who are reading this remarkable man for the first time, you will find entering the world of Frank Mele a great treat.

—NICK LYONS
New York, 1988

Frank Mele died in 1996.

SMALL IN THE EYE OF A RIVER

BLUE DUN

IT IS NATURAL, I think, for beginnings to be arbitrary. Even human lives, it seems, can begin somewhat capriciously. Any account of inceptions is therefore apt to be treacherous, or at best unreliable—especially so if one seeks for causes to satisfy the human prerequisite to Effect. How to enter into even the merest thumbnail history of an attitude compounded from flowing waters, bankside dawdlers, bamboo, cock's hackles, and a certain color of intermediate hue, and to give some intimation of their genesis, is a task for wiser heads than mine.

I suppose I could say, for example, that the glowing vision of a Blue Dun cape materialized one night as my pregnant mother knelt at prayer before her little Madonna. But this would be sheer fabrication, and even worse an affront to the quality of her fervor, for she wanted her unborn son to be a violinist. In her frame of mind, the Blue Dun cape would have been taken for some harping angel in miniature, or a biblical dove with Blue Dun feathers appropriate to the sky of Heaven.

Now, all this might ingratiate me to the good folks of the world but I would be answerable to the few who know that it is from just such compromises that many a potent myth has had its start. Caught thus, between the half-truths of our salty worthies and the gem-hard unpleasantries of the few, I could try to salvage some of my peace of mind by affirming that since myths appear to be as necessary as breathing to the run-of-the-mill of the species, I shall not try to discredit them, since, by acquiescing to that grand old custom, there is the chance of an absolution of anglers. In other words, if what is sauce for the goose, et cetera, there is no longer ground for casting aspersions on anglers. And no need to take their redemption any farther. For all that anglers' myths tend to fragility they are still a good deal less vulnerable than the contrivances of ordinary men. I trust that now I can get on with the narrative without ransacking my racial memory for some specious cause—say, an angling ancestor who might justify the events to follow.

There was little in my childhood that might have cast any significant shadows before, unless it was a predilection for puddles. Later, in boyhood, when great and sudden rainstorms magically transformed the city streets into brooks, an unexplainable ecstasy would drive me out of doors to hover dreamy-eyed about the curbstone banks of the new rivulets. To this day, when a muskrat clambers out to some riverbank, I am reminded of the rats that scrambled out of the flooded sewer drains and went scurrying over the great cobblestones of the street.

Some years later, done with early studies, well past the intermediate stage, and reeking with the faint, musty odor of the mud, weeds, and pickerel of the farmland streams near my native Rochester, I went to Syracuse to find new ways for scaling the higher reaches of violin playing. That I had already been one of the youngest members of the Rochester Philharmonic Orchestra did not seem to me as impressive, honorable, or profitable as to have the inner beauty of a musical phrase revealed to me by a gaunt and profane master, Andre Polsh, my teacher, an artist of stature—one of the elect, whose career had been stifled by an ironic accident.

An ominous silence had settled over the nation. And when in its deepest recesses, a cataclysmic bomb exploded, shattering the national economy, the country reeled and staggered in a state of shock. Life went on, but with empty pockets and, quite often, an empty belly—that is, among the laboring classes and those of us in the arts. And when, against the protestations and vilifications of outraged Pilgrims, who had acquired affluence presumably without the help of God, a crippled and compassionate President decreed the Work Projects, we musicians filed due notice of bona fide indigence, cut the fringes from our trouser cuffs, and began to use our professional skills as members of the new symphony orchestra. It was held to be one of the more contemptible projects, in that men were getting paid, however minimally, for merely making great music.

Andre was a gifted conductor as well, and when he was appointed director of the orchestra he set about reconciling his passion for a high standard of performance, as much as his choleric nature would permit, with the inevitable quota of mediocrities that were better suited to vaudeville than to Mozart, Brahms, Debussy, and yes, even Stravinsky. There was now relief from want, but not from the humiliation that attended its formalities; and what shreds of dignity had survived the stigma attached to the projects were annihilated by a jibing press and the indignation of the good burghers of upper New York State. Those were gloomy days, scarcely relieved by the pall of grime that hung over the scabrous public buildings. The drabness of that city was exceeded only by a pervasive meanness of spirit. But redemption could be found in the beauty of its country-side. Out beyond the green drumlins, among the valleys to the northeast and south, beautiful streams with Indian names beckoned, inviting heavy hearts to lightness, and corroded hopes to a good burnishing at the hands of waterside alders.

Andre was a fly fisher, and when this mad Dutchman adopted me as his fishing companion, my hopes began to soar, as an early zeal for bait casting got transposed to the fly rod. As in violin playing, I sought out the masters, ransacking the shelves of the university and public libraries for books on fly fishing. In the stacks I found Emlyn Gill, Bergman, Hewitt, Southard, Lord Grey. I saved enough to send to Paul Young for his *Making and Using the Fly and Leader.* And then I began to tie flies, buying books by the dozen, when I could afford them. Certain exotic materials could only be purchased.

Others I begged. And many I borrowed from an environment that had taken on a new depth. A rich world of texture and color had opened to me. For the first time I saw the extraordinary range of color in dogs, cats, pet and wild rabbits, monkeys, mice, squirrels, ducks, geese, and fowl of all kinds. My visits to the zoo now had a vibrant urgency that gave pause to children and made the keepers nervous. And when the orchestra played at a county fair that was famous for its yearly exhibit of rare fowl, and I found the attendant away for lunch, my head swam. In the operation that followed, a dizziness nearly overcame me, fearing that at any moment the uproar would fetch a guard.

One morning at rehearsal, a new man came in dragging a cello by the scruff of the neck. Andre had briefed me about him over the previous day's intermission coffee. In the excitement, Andre's English, normally unpredictable, had slipped a few cogs and was being ground up by Dutch, French, and German accents. Under those great eyebrows of Holland straw, his blue eyes were gleaming wolfishly. In a gravelly bass he told me the news. "This man is un maker of rodts! Un goddamt specialiste von fly rodts! Dry-fly rodts!" I could not have been more impressed had Andre announced the entry of Pablo Casals into our ranks. Our rods were of poor quality, soft as willow. Andre's treasured rods and reels by Hardy had been stolen from his car years ago.

Andre's words were still reverberating in my ear as Dan Brenan took his place at the rear of the cello section. As he began to tune his cello he looked so unprofessional that I began to get faintly sick. But shortly I saw something that made me close my eyes in blessed relief. There would not be, could not be, any repercussion from the podium. Hopelessly out of practice after years of rodmaking, Brenan had sacked valor for a plausible discretion. It would have been difficult for him to have made an audible mistake. He was bowing away impassively, in step with the others, the bow hair hovering over the treacherous rapids then settling down agreeably in the more navigable runs, glides, and pools. It was a stroke of true wisdom, appreciated none the less by Andre than by me. One day, Brenan invited me to his shop.

Coming in to the warmth of a little world of bamboo out of the whiplashing snows and icy sidewalks of Syracuse was no less than a bit of parochial magic, bringing easement and balm to a troubled soul. The shop's mood was a melange of violin-maker's shop and tackle store, sources both for repose and wonder. There I saw and fondled my first dry-fly rods. Had Brenan had an apprenticeship or a family tradition there would not have been any flaw of workmanship. If imperfect, they were superb in action; I have had a few others in hand since then that were comparable to his best rods, and many that were inferior. However prudent a cellist, Dan was an adventurous rodmaker; and in the matter of rod design for the dry fly he was ahead of his time.

A blackboard with the chalked heading, DAYS TO OPENING DAY, read 63, awaiting the first of the coterie to come in to roost out of the waning afternoon, leaving the gloom, chill, and snow to the defeated day. By five-thirty the blackboard read 62. I basked in the warmth of talk that diverted the winter stream to its summer course on the shop's floor. Rods sprang to life. Lines darted and looped under the soiled sky of the ceiling. At a bench to one side sat Bill, Dan's son, at his after-work vise, contriving a better bivisible fly than the last. Flies whisked about. A great trout rose to McBride's fly of last summer, then plunged downward to sulk in the depths of the floor below. It was the rite of the Waiting Men enduring their season of work with invocations to a reluctant spring—not a whit less primitive than the crude and basic formalities of their remote ancestors. From a judicial chamber, from a locomotive's cab, from symphony hall, office, machine shop, barroom, laboratory, they had come to improvise upon their truth, which was the Dry Fly.

Later, at a nearby tavern, Dan, mellowing in whisky, would hold forth for the hardier few. A gifted writer on many aspects of the sport, Dan had an extensive correspondence with leading figures in the field. His knowledge of the angling history of the Catskill and Adirondack mountains was imposing and intimate; and the names I culled out of those benign extemporizations sounded like a roll call of latter-day saints: Theodore Gordon, La Branche, Hewitt, Holden, of the *Idyll of the Split Bamboo,* Izaak Walton (no less a figure than Dante), Halford, the English Prince of the True Faith, and then the glorious school of Catskill fly tyers who had received Gordon's afflatus at death: Reuben Cross, Herman Christian, the Darbees, Walt Dette. By now Dan had become for me the arbiter of all things piscatorial, and an inexhaustible source of fishing lore.

One afternoon at the tavern Dan had soared to really admirable form, and was weaving in and out of the key of Dry Fly Major with the skill of an Irish Bach when, at once, he struck an arresting chord. "The Quill Gordon fly," said Dan, "was the great turning point in American dry-fly fishing. Gordon's creativity in his choice of materials and his ingenuity in determining a just style for our waters set the pattern that was to become our tradition. After an extensive correspondence with the mighty Halford, and a cordial exchange of flies he departed once and for all from the English tradition, retaining only that which could be adapted to his concept of a fly that could dance on our broken waters, and which, on our long glides and pools, looked like a newly hatched dun. It is therefore *de rigueur*, mandatory, that this fly be tied with the natural Blue Dun hackle! Else it is not a true Quill Gordon fly!" By now Dan's voice had the ring of One Hundred Proof. "For that matter," he added, "no fly could rightfully bear the name Dun unless it was tied in the natural color!"

There it was. With four words Dan had wakened me out of a deep sleep, only to plunge me into a nightmare of frustration at the thought of all those Quill Gordon flies I had tied from a very well dyed cock's neck of excellent quality. I had traded a pernambuco violin bow for it to a greedy dealer in fly-tying materials. The fact that the bow was not a true pernambuco was small consolation. The neck was not a true Blue Dun. Dan's words resolved all doubts that I had from time to time about those flies. Their color was inert. They reminded me of ash. Dan's incantation had at once set me before the Veil that concealed a great Mystery. What the revelation could conceivably be was as yet only a strange stirring of blood in my head. This color, Blue Dun, would I know it were I to come suddenly face to face with it? What could there be about it which had set it apart so remotely yet compellingly on a mountain peak in my mind?

"Well, Frankie," said Dan. "I can only say that there is nothing quite like it. I don't know how to describe it. One simply has to see the natural Blue Dun for himself, with his own eyes. Only then can he understand. It is one of Nature's rare moods. It is color and light making their ways out of chaos and darkness." For the moment I had to content myself with this Hibernian tune from the Prophet. Had Dan had access then to Gordon's letters to the great English angler, G.E.M. Skues, he would have quoted:

"My farmer friend and I have been trying to breed good dun hackles, but the cocks are turning out poorly."

Later: "I found a blue cock of the year yesterday and hope that I will succeed in buying the bird—the neck is of such a lovely color."

And six years later: "It seems too bad when we consider how rarely one finds a cock with blue dun hackles." Even then, it seems, the natural color was painfully scarce.

Dan, I am sure, was not aware of what was happening to me, else he would have modified his dictum from unalterable law to permissible deviation. He had a deep respect for my skill as a violinist, and a personal liking that probably set me only a cut or two below Theodore Gordon, for Dan adored great music. But I do believe that had he altered his *pronunciamiento* out of care for my peace of mind, and that of my family's, I doubt that it would have greatly diverted the course of the future. Blue Dun was now a fever in my brain.

The violence of my reaction and its later consequences cannot be entirely ascribed to Dan, with all due respect to his eloquence and imagery. Later events tend to suggest that the occasion triggered something deep within, well beyond normal reach, well to the other side of any intimation, even, of its existence; for I had yet to see a single feather of natural Blue Dun.

Then, streambound early one Sunday morning, as the car was hurtling over the road, the irascible Marcel gave me what appears now to be the first lucid description of the color Blue Dun. This taut but admirable Frenchman, a hairdresser, was a passionate angler whose fly casting was a model of elegance and precision. He was singing obscene French songs, by way, I thought, of exorcising the previous day's ordeal with fat and fretful matrons. When he had finished still another classic of the latrine, I put the question to him. He was a knowledgeable and meticulous fly tyer.

"Marcel. What is the real Blue Dun like? The natural—you know—"

"Ah, *mon cher,*" he replied. "That? What can I say? It is like nothing else, and everything. It is not blue, like the flag blue. It is something that is always—how shall I say? Becoming?"

Late that afternoon at Marcel's home I saw my first natural Blue Dun neck. I was silent a long time. It was real, and it was there. But it was unreal, and it was somewhere else. Marcel was right. It was in the act of becoming. I raised my eyes at last and spoke.

"Marcel. Where is Blue Dun?"

"Ah." Marcel canted his head a bit to one side. "That is a difficult question. How shall I tell you? That is where you find it? Yes. To find it. Until then it is like the—like the smoke—"

"In search of the sky."

"Yes! Exactly!" Marcel nodded sharply, then suddenly fixed me with a curious look followed by an expression of bewilderment, as of a spirit scurrying through the ages.

"But how did you know?" he asked, from a great distance.

"I'm not sure," I said, my words sounding from afar. "You may have said it once before, and I remembered it."

Hairdressers, I believe, are masters of applied psychology. Marcel had read something in my face that was unintentional, of which I was not aware.

"What size do you tie the Quill Gordon?" he asked.

"Twelve."

He riffled affectionately through the quivering hackles, then carefully plucked out two and gave them to me. It was an act of superlative generosity, well beyond friendship. I had heard it said that the French were stingy. I say that they are selectively extravagant. On that occasion it was nothing less than a minor sacrifice, which only a cynic can make without pomp. *"Bon!"* concluded Marcel. "You are now fit to enter the Beaverkill. You are going next week with Dan?"

"Yes. Dan is taking three of us. It will be my very first time. I have never seen it, except in dreams."

"Ah," sighed Marcel. "It is a dream within a dream."

On a fresh summer morning a week later, as Blue Dun was rising in the east, a Ford went wheezing toward the valleys where the sacred rivers ran. Under the wise and gentle guidance of Dan, the Prophet, three of us were to have our baptism at last in the Beaverkill River.

Hours later, when the southern hills had greatened to Catskill massiveness, we descended a long, winding grade and the Ford stopped, heaving and burbling in exhaustion at the bank of a majestic pool. We alighted. The Prophet turned to us, intoned the keynote and conducted an impromptu cantata, the hymn, "Praise God from Whom All Blessings Flow." It was an unlikely chorus: a nominal Protestant, a fled Catholic, a remoted Jew, and an atheist. But it was in tune, and fervent. In a many-celled fly box, squatting in its own special compartment, the fly with the mystical color listened, awaiting its first flight over the holy waters.

If memory serves me, and often it doesn't, we camped near to the Mountain Pool. Darkness was nigh, and wood was fetched at Dan's request for a fire big enough to conjure up the Spirits of the River, that he might transpose the secrets that passed back and forth from the distant rapids to the crackling flames. As the night deepened, the thin, reedy chords of a harmonica floated in and out of the conversational murmur. It was a nostalgic whimper before the fact of smallness beneath a firmament of start—the Aeolian harp of the Catskills singing of humility and peace, and gratitude to the great Unknown.

Later, two figures materialized from the outer world of darkness and entered the glow of the fire to bring their hands to Dan's. Gladness and surprise were in the Prophet's greetings, and through their fullness there ran a finely gleaming thread of respect. One of them was Reuben Cross, the greathearted and improvident master of fly making who was already a legend, and with him was Alfred W. Miller, the Sparse Grey Hackle of the genial writings that were enriching Beaverkill lore.

In the early morning I entered the waters, rod in hand. I do not remember how many trout rose to my fly—or whether, indeed, any did. But I shall not forget that I moved as in a dream, hearing the voices of the river rising and falling with mysterious clarity through the hovering mists. And I remember the crystalline water that seemed to magnify the purity of the rocks, and the cool green darkness of the ferns, a profusion of frail, lush arches in the shadowed banks; and as the mist began to rise, a doe and her fawn crossed the pool below.

In the ensuing years, my work as a symphonist took me to various parts of the country for the fall, winter, and spring months. As each music season rounded its peak, and spring was faintly visible in the distant valley, the voice of a wakened obsession would begin loudening to a command to action. The trail was faint, often washed out. But, like a stubborn hound I would return to certain crossways, hoping for a cold scent that would lead miraculously to a Blue Dun cape of quality that had fallen asleep in mid-flight. When the orchestra played *The Moldau,* a tone poem which the Bohemian Smetana had distilled from the sounds of a great river, my left-hand fingers would scurry agreeably with the riffles at its headwaters, but the bow had become a fly rod in the other hand. The fly was, appropriately, a Blue Dun, since I had long ago formulated the theory that the natural Dun-hackled fly would take trout anywhere in the world at one time or another.

On nights off, a few of us would meet to play chamber music. The music we made, mostly for ourselves, was the most rewarding of all in terms of personal fulfillment. And if a pianist and a bassist were present, no great persuasion was needed for them to join us in a reading of Schubert's *Trout Quintet,* a tribute to that noble fish by the Austrian genius. As in the song that had inspired the Quintet, the measured buoyant cheer of its theme would have been perfect incidental music to the ballet of a stately brown swirling at his feast of mayfly nymphs aspiring to dunhood. Later, in the quiet of the Pittsburgh night, I would write another of those ritual letters—this time to a house in England: "Gentlemen, would you by chance have a cock's cape of natural Blue Dun of good quality to offer? I am aware of the rarity of this color and am, accordingly, prepared to consider the payment of a premium. I would be most grateful . . ."

I suppose it was inevitable that I should one day settle in the Catskills. I had had as much as I wanted of the unquiet life, and one year I returned, not merely for the summer, but to stay, in a village within twenty minutes' drive of the Esopus, a river proud and mighty still, its spirit unbroken after years of torment by water-greedy Manhattan. My community had a rich and highly respected tradition of the arts, offering scope for playing in a summer series of distinction and a likely potential for students of the violin and viola. Then, within one to two hours' reach there flowed the great rivers of angling history, allegedly tired, but still alluring and productive in their classically temperamental fashion. These were the Schoharie, the Delawares, East and West, the Willowemoc, and the Neversink and Beaverkill rivers.

My decision, however, had come at a time when, for perhaps too many reasons, mind and body had wandered off into a twilight world. There is a withering hostility in the winter Catskills, a taut suspension of life outdoors that can drive men's backs against their own walls. There is beauty, too; and joy may be found or contrived. But the gnawings of a marginal life can dispose a man toward the consolations of the jug. The cheapness and goodness of native applejack made it possible to appease a growing congenital thirst, transporting me to an inner island so beguiling that I did not want to leave. I was unable to. Years drifted by. Then, shambling one day through the familiar vapors, I stumbled over my persistent little man again, the one I had ignored and even insulted so often in the past. This time I heard him out: I believed him, and together we managed to stop it once and for all. I did not know it then, but he was congenital, too.

As I improved, I began reconstituting the sport, and shortly began to hear the distant crowing of Blue Dun roosters again. The awakening was owing in part to the interest and kindness of Preston Jennings, who had recently retired to nearby Bearsville. His classic *A Book of Trout Flies* was, for me, the first truly significant work on angling entomology and dry-fly design for Eastern streams. It brought order to the chaos of a still rather wayward tradition of American dry-fly fishing and carried it to solid ground. It was issued in a limited edition by a private press in elegant format and was, ironically, remaindered. Its cost at the time was one factor. The other may have been the cool objectivity of a style uninviting to those American anglers who were still disposed toward boyish writings on fishing. However, by now the book had reemerged as a rare find, commanding premium prices—and it was very scarce. All told, it amounted very nearly to a conspiracy. Accordingly, Jennings was not awarded the honor due him in his lifetime.

His genius is reflected in another work, the *Streamside Guide,* by Arthur Flick; and Jennings may be said to have been god-father to this indispensable little book.

Curiously, I found that Jennings' passion for the stream had also entered a state of suspension, although unlike mine, his was marked by sobriety, tinged however, with disillusion. Some causes for the latter have been implied. Then, too, Bobby was a man of sensibility, intelligence, and aesthetic awareness, all of which together can incline one to vulnerability. Such persons must stand on reserve or perish, at risk of incurring a judgment of pride. But such was not the case, and I like to think that I may have played a small part in his reconciliation to the Catskill streams, for which I think he was glad, or so it seemed as I watched him flexing his beloved Payne rod over a riffle-head, proving the potency of his Blue Dun Variant in conjuring a fifteen-inch brown out of its depths.

At his home one evening, Bobby brought out a small box and opened it with a reverence suggestive of a collector opening to some fabulous diamond. In it were dry flies which had been tied by Herman Christian and Theodore Gordon. I could not imagine them more perfect had they been tied that morning. One of the original models for the Quill Gordon fly was among them. Its form and color engraved themselves in my mind and thereafter became the model for my own imitations. I have since seen other flies allegedly by Gordon, but none had the finesse or the buoyant elegance.

As a tyer, Bobby was a superior artist, and his materials were the finest I had ever seen, or have ever seen since. Among his necks were Blue Duns as fine as I ever hope to see. Jennings was also inclined to the artist's brush and palette, and I believe that this together with a related color-study, in which he had been absorbed for some time, had drawn him and his gracious wife to an artistic environment. His experience with salmon flies while fishing the great coastal rivers of the East had led to an inquiry into the reasons for the effectiveness of the many-hued salmon fly; and that to a study of the prismatic effect given off by the tiny bubbles of air formed about the microscopic filaments or hairs on the body of a rising nymph. Further inquiry had suggested that the salmon's memory held an indelible association of these colors with the food nymphs of its grilsehood. All told, his efforts had begun to yield up a logical case for the salmon fly and its seemingly irrational gaudiness.

I felt pleased, even honored by Jennings' friendship, but in a rather vague, disembodied way. For those were difficult days—days in which the slow withdrawal of the alcohol had brought to view the shambles of a once productive life, and of a collective fruitfulness reduced to abject singleness. Vaguely aware of trudging forward, I was mostly conscious of a mouthful of ashes, of a battered spirit which had barely averted bankruptcy. But, as I have since gathered, my outer aspect was one of calm bordering on indifference, occasionally rising to arrogance. How far this was from the actual inward state would be a volume in itself, a compact little book, some of whose contents Bobby may have discerned: for one evening, in his studio, as he was delving into a drawer, he turned suddenly to me with a smile. In his outstretched hand was a superb cape of natural

Blue Dun. For reasons that have never been clear I declined it, with a thick murmur of thanks. I doubt whether I could have offended him more. I had virtually spit into the face of a noble gesture, one prompted by the purest motive of intuitive sensibility. Apparently, my reconstruction still had a long way to go. It is not surprising then, that after an unfortunate misunderstanding, we never saw each other again.

An offer came from an orchestra in Texas. Glad for the opportunity of relief from the aftermath of recent history, I accepted. Far from the Catskills, far from trout, my bewildered fly rods huddling in a friend's closet, I entered into the symphonic world again under the benevolent auspices of a mild Texas winter. But when the last Norther had subsided to spring, the old song of the quest began humming in my head again—and the voices of the rivers that flowed under the distant silhouettes of my mountains. I began to write letters that were utterly incongruous with that flat and surly land: "Gentlemen, would you by chance—Blue Dun? I would be most grateful—"

Returned to a comparatively tranquil and ordered life in the Catskills, I found it necessary from time to time to suspend the attrition of the long, bitter winters with occasional jaunts to Jerusalem. Together with my angling companions of some years we found respite from the winter jitters by observing, from time to time, one of a number of what may be called "Darbee Days." I suppose that, given other circumstances, they may have been called "Walt Dette," "Bill Kelly," or "Roy Steenrod" Days, for they, too, were a part of the angling-conservation custodianship at the banks of the great tradition. They were the Keepers of the Gate. But the Darbees were friends of long standing; and then—well yes, there was also the little matter of their Blue Dun fowl, a strain of their own breeding that glared peevishly out of the many cages in the back yard. Inside, we basked in the homemade sunlight of hackles, hooks, furs, rods, reels, lines, leaders, nets; selecting materials with which to tie flies at home later, by way of preserving our sanities during the deserted time of the year. There was talk of flies, of streams, of the men who lived for them, of books in which the waters ran, and where now and then one found a superior music which had been inspired by the trout, a simple vertebrate, but with this difference: That it stirred a mystery in the deepest recesses of our beings, a primal nostalgia that quickened in the sight of its brilliant spots and bands of iridescence where gulps of moonlight had congealed to color. Padding in with feminine unobtrusiveness, the First Lady of American fly tying gave greeting and passed to some other phase of sorting. Held by some to be, craftwise, the better half of the Darbee legend, Elsie would have disdained and Harry confirmed it. Actually, the differences, if any, were beyond the ken of niggling amateurs. Above the genial drone of Harry's voice on the trial of a point of conservation there sounded the faint, rhythmical fanfare of Blue Dun cocks, proud in their little beaked trumpets.

Later, on the long drive home, fly life hatched and surfaced in the murmuring car, and the unheard litanies to a reluctant spring that sang under our words must surely have been noted under the thick ice of Pepacton Reservoir and commented upon with frigid bubbles by the huge trout which had greatened in it within a few miles of its source, the self-renouncing Delaware.

Came the fall of another year, and Fate took one of us for a disastrous ride. For two weeks Jim Mulligan lay in a coma. Waking, he was to lie for two years in a veterans hospital bed until the one half of his body could support the paralyzed half. How many connivances and fabrications that Joe Nazzaro and I dreamed up en route to the hospital I cannot remember; nor how many precious days of liberty that Joe, and I, too, gave up that we might bring the stream to the distant bedside where our shattered friend lay.

But mercy, however capricious, will also have its say; and in having regained the use of one half of his body, Jim, a distinguished cartoonist, set himself the formidable task of transferring the skill of a now inert hand to the strong but untrained one. There came a winter's day at last when the inroads of "cabin fever" decreed a Darbee Day. Once again, with our valiant but unsteady Jim, we set off on wings of Blue Dun.

At Margaretville we crossed the upper Delaware and shortly were following the shoreline road of the severely beautiful Pepacton. Later, turning away from the reservoir, we began the long ascent, then down to Roscoe; and when we crossed the upper Beaverkill I doffed the only hat for the three of us. Shortly beyond the village, on the Manor road, we skirted the Willowemoc, green-bubbling at its icy lips and winter dark in the upper pool. In the riffles above, a cold fire flared under a shaft of brilliant sunlight from a rift in the gray clouds.

Time has not perceptibly dimmed my memory of Darbee's greeting to the man whom destiny had banged on the brain; nor the implication that it had done so ineffectively. Out the candor of his blue eyes, out the heart of a rich experience, came the blessing of man's humility to man: a beckoning to Jim to search and find a wholeness of his own. Before we left, he gave Jim the token that would articulate his wish for many a year. It was in a paper sack.

As the car was cantering home along the Pepacton road Jim opened the paper sack with his good hand. In the waning light of the afternoon we saw the Blue Dun cape glowing. As he turned it we saw the component glints in the light from the reflecting whiteness of the reservoir. Visibly moved by his great good fortune, Jim's speech, till now painfully laborious, made a curious modulation and he said, slowly but clearly, "It seems to have other meanings."

In my cabinet of fly materials there is a special drawer. Lying in it are a small number of Blue Dun capes of varying shades nestling about each other in all the glory of their muted iridescence. They were all acquired more or less honorably: that is, in the sense that legitimacy and honesty are terms subject to parochial rules, and that it takes a good deal of imagination to transcend our little moral geographies.

I will not say how many there are, because I want to be surprised every time I count them. And when I do so, it is less to affirm my possessiveness than the privilege of their custody. That they are only a small part of countless numbers of shades and attitudes of color piques me, but it does not disturb me, for the ones allotted to me all have their special meaning. Each is a memento of a particular quest. They invite, of course, to other quests, but I really need not undertake them, because each day the colors are a little bit different, as each day is different; and thus they multiply in my mind's eye. Through their difference as in the multicolored variants of Bach's great *Chaconne,* there runs the somber strain of the fact that I grow older, and soon the fiddle strings will fray out and their sound must fade. But the colors will not, for Blue Dun waits upon other questions, whose answers, even more than mine, will disavow finality. As for instance, "Why is Blue Dun?"

One could as well ask: "Why is Love?" Or, indeed, "Why is Life?"

A FISHING TALE

ANGLING TENDS to round a man out, but in a way quite different from potatoes and beer: It adds dimension to his ability to carry out his tasks. True, it also tends to make a man contentious; but this is only a minor part of his total awareness of himself, and of Immortality. The imminence of a Myth—with a fish, that is—has put a grave responsibility upon him which will explain his severity in piscatorial matters.

There are instances in which this rounding out, together with a certain maturing of the mind, sets a man apart from his fellows. Such a man was the Honorable Elias Meltzer (may the Lord rest his soul), Justice of the United States District Court, whose decisions, many of which are now legal history, allowed for no compromises with his passion for law and order.

Most of what I know about Judge Meltzer I learned from his son, Samuel, my angling companion of many years with whom I'd shared many a reach of classic Catskill water, and other streams less famous and best known to ourselves.

Sam's mother had passed away prematurely, leaving him, however, to the best of fathers, one whose humanitarianism and moral disciplines were firmly integrated into the warp and weft of his paternal love.

The Judge was one of the best anglers of an older school, one that calls to mind the saints of early fly fishing, such as Gordon, Hewitt, La Branche, and the other greats, less literary but no less accomplished. In the club to which the Judge belonged he was held in respect that amounted nearly to awe. Among his many qualities as angler he possessed that indefinable instinct known as "trout sense." Men who are born with it have the ability to "read water," an intuitive faculty which, at best, amounts to an uncanny ability to locate trout. When necessary, the Judge could stand motionless as a heron for long periods of time; and when it was time to present the fly his casting was well-nigh flawless.

These qualities the Judge began to pass on to his son at an early age; and I would surmise, from my observations of Sam, the adult angler, that the Judge had had a pupil worthy of the Master.

After his graduation from Princeton University, Sam was offered a minor executive position with a large corporation where his intelligence, imagination, and dedication to work earned him a series of promotions in short order. His only fault, if it may be called that, was a firmly rooted sense of honesty that made his superiors—and now these were few—a bit uneasy. Under Sam's managership the flood of returns of defective merchandise had dwindled to practically nothing. This was unsettling to the modernists about him because it had also reduced the margin of profits; but it would have been unthinkable to let him go. Those bright, new ratings now being given the corporation by consumers' testing groups were heady stuff. They gave tone and distinction; they gave the other executives the illusion that they, too, had integrity. Sam's colleagues voted to raise him to a vice-presidency instead, sending him off to manage the European branch. By this time the Judge had retired, and was casting about for a place where he could pass the remaining years of his life, close to his beloved sport.

Before leaving for Europe, Sam had the satisfaction of seeing his father very much at home in an old, but well-preserved stone farmhouse which was set on a rise overlooking a pastoral valley along which there wound a crystal-clear, cool, slow-moving stream. It was one of those rare, unspoiled limestone streams such as may be occasionally found in Pennsylvania or central New York. The farm was really quite extensive, giving the Judge nearly half a mile of stream which had been closely preserved over the years.

Directly below the house the stream widened, giving the effect of a narrow little pond. There, as in the narrower reaches, traceries of weeds gave assurance of ample food and cover for both brown and native brook trout. The latter, while not as large or numerous as the browns, had managed to hold their own very well.

Sam was looking forward eagerly to his new duties in Europe and, I could well imagine, his fishing holidays on the trout waters of England, France, and Austria. His anticipation was marred, however, by certain reservations about his beloved father. But after he arrived, a brisk correspondence with the old Judge put his mind at ease.

In the second year of Sam's European stay his father's letters began to make allusions to a certain trout who lived in his stream. Apparently, this trout had become a pet of his which, for some curious reason, the Judge had named Delfino. Sam often wondered how Delfino, Italian for dolphin, could apply to a trout. It suggested a playful nature and a high degree of intelligence.

The Judge's summer letters made frequent mention of Delfino. "When another trout takes my fly," said one letter, "he resents it a great deal, and you'd hardly believe the commotion. He might go on punishing that trout until—well, he banishes him for days." On another occasion the Judge wrote, "He got so angry when Blueback (a large native brook trout) took my Red Quill that he raised the dickens with him all over the pool. I can't imagine how, but evidently in the scuffle he got the fly away from him. Anyway, he had it . . ."

At about this stage Sam began to have his doubts about the solitary life his father was leading. Other references to Delfino that followed in the ensuing year had so intensified the unreality of the matter as to suggest that the old man's experience had strayed beyond the limits of eccentricity into hallucination.

Toward the end of Sam's four-year stay he began to feel some uneasiness at the thought of reunion with his father. Deep in his mind there lurked a fear of finding his father a helpless victim to the corrosion of old age, teetering helplessly between hallucination and the babblings of second childhood.

That first drive to the farmhouse after his return was one of the most trying experiences in Sam's life. Fearing the worst, he was greeted instead with unabashed affection by a father whose lucidity and verve were as much a source of astonishment and delight as of relief. After dinner Sam asked about the fish. A smile dawned over the Judge's face until it was luminous with pleasure.

"You wouldn't know Delfino now," he said.

"But Dad," said Sam, "I've never seen him."

"Oh yes, you have," nodded the Judge. "Do you remember the week before you left? A nice brown had taken your fly, and while you were playing him a larger one was following him around?"

"Oh," said Sam. "Him?"

"Yes. That was Delfino. You'll see him later."

After supper the Judge went over to a rack where a number of fly rods were standing and selected one.

"This is the one he likes best," said the Judge. Sam remembered the rod very well. Of odd length, slightly over seven feet, it had been made to the Judge's order by that great artist among rodmakers, James Payne.

As they sauntered down the field toward the stream, Sam noticed that his father was not wearing a fishing vest nor had he brought a fly box for spare flies.

"Dad," he said, "you've only got that one fly on your leader."

The Judge nodded. "That's all I need. You'll see."

It was a well-nigh perfect summer evening. The air had cooled but was still soft, without a hint of oppressiveness. Some birds were already swooping over the wide water of the stream; evidently, a hatch had begun. As they approached the bankside the Judge pointed upstream where a riffle from the current above was playing and spending itself in the pool.

"They've started," said the Judge. Sam saw the rings forming at the tail of the riffle, widening toward the quieter water. Then, as if at a signal, the rising stopped.

"That's Delfino," said the Judge. "He saw me and he's taking his place. That's why they stopped. He's driven them off."

The Judge had scarcely finished when a solitary rise bulged the surface slightly, creating rings that spread with a leisurely and somewhat proprietary roll.

Now, I've recalled much of what Sam had told me, with, I think, fair fidelity; but that which followed is so remarkable that, rather than risk suspicion of any misinterpretation on my part, I will take it verbatim from the tape recording I made of Sam when he told it one evening:

My father now began working the line out until the fly was flirting over the fish, and in the next cast he let the fly drop just a bit to one side of the rise. I really don't think the fly had alighted when there was a great upheaval, the line darted forward and then—well—that was Delfino.

Now, after those years of separation and correspondence, Dad was, perhaps a little eager to show me this prodigy of his, so that when Delfino overreacted, as he did, Dad reacted likewise—a most unusual thing for him—and he struck too hard.

As I saw him stripping in the line trailing the flyless leader, I offered to go up to the house for one of his fly boxes.

"No. Not at all," said Dad. "Just come along with me, and don't make any sudden movements." I followed him carefully to a little cove where the stream-bottom sloped upwards, then leveled off to about ten inches of water at the bank. Here Dad squatted at the very edge. "Just watch this," he said.

As my eyes wandered out from the little cove into the pool I saw a dark shape materializing out of the dark green and cruising toward the cove. As it approached rising towards the surface, I saw the spots becoming clearer until, in the light from the setting sun, they stood out in all their brilliant color on a brown trout which I estimated to be 25 to 26 inches in length.

To this day there are times when that which followed takes on a dreamlike quality, and something or someone inside me begins insisting that it happened in sleep. You will understand why.

The great trout now glided with slow dignity into the cove and I saw that his mouth was opening and closing. Then I saw the fly.

Delfino saw me, and it seemed that there was doubt and disapproval in his eye. As he wavered I saw Dad's fingers working through the surface film with a gentle, rubbing motion. Delfino swam forward, and with a gentle, deft motion, Dad plucked the fly out of his mouth. At once I understood the ease of it. The hook was barbless. Delfino turned and swam off into the pool.

As in a dream I saw my father threading the fly to the leader again, squeezing it dry in an old bandanna as we walked to our former stand at the bank. Within a minute a portly, bubbling rise signaled Delfino's return to his post. Again my father began to lengthen his cast, dropping the fly in, very nearly, the same place.

But, curiously, this time there was no commotion. As the fly vanished into the little whirlpool, Dad merely raised the rod, setting the hook with deliberation. Delfino began racing from one side of the pool to the other. It struck me now that he could have chosen to plunge into any one of a number of weedbeds. But he didn't. Deliberately, it seemed, he had chosen to fight rather near the surface, creating wakes that made my heart beat quite fast.

I said fight, but really it was something else. Delfino tore all over the pool, but his actions were never frantic. However, he did break water twice, making the whole pool tremble and, judging by his size, I was now prepared to wait a half hour or more. But after his second leap and a few more runs Delfino appeared to be losing strength or, as it transpired, what passed for it.

Keeping a steady but unstrained arch to his rod, Dad began walking slowly toward the cove where he stopped and waited. Shortly he began reeling in and it was not long before the great fish sailed into the cove, his nose within three feet of the bank, showing not the slightest sign of exhaustion.

My father now raised his rod until Delfino's back was showing out of the water and slowly coaxed him to the edge of the bank. Dad squatted down, and as Delfino's nose came out of the water I heard Dad shout:

"Dead fish!"

Once again, he commanded:

"Dead fish!"

A curious, rather filmy look came over Delfino's eye and he began to wobble unsteadily from one side to the other. Suddenly he made a complete roll and stood still, his great, white belly turned toward the sky. As Dad reached for the fly he turned, looked up at me with—I scarcely know how to describe it. The closest thing I can think of was that it was an expression of pure transport in which there was playing a smile of nearly childlike pride and joy.

Now, I am as aware as the next man of the great human potential and the marvels of human ingenuity. But I question whether we shall ever approach, in any mechanistic way, that innate, incredible faculty in all of us which, in an instant, can recall an entire lifetime. In that instant, on that memorable evening on the stream, all that I had known of my father's life flashed at once and I wondered: Was this the man who had taken influential politicians to task? Who had sent the Mayor of a large city to prison for fraud? Who had, against threats to his life, sentenced the leader of a powerful crime syndicate to hard labor for life? And together with him, half the policemen of a notorious precinct?

Now came one of those rare and precious insights which become the cornerstones of a man's wisdom. Yes, indeed, it was the same man. It had to be, precisely because of this. I saw at the very heart of jurisprudence how judges were as great as their custodianship of Man's nobler qualities. As never before, I understood the greatness of the man whose fingers were fondly tickling the belly of his great trout (Delfino's tail was quivering ecstatically). For Elias Meltzer, Man's greatest offense was the forfeiture of his innocence.

I was quite unprepared for what followed: Delfino gave a sudden, convulsive heave, coming partly out of the water, his tail gave a powerful thrust and he was off. Dad was upright now, his face and clothes utterly drenched. May God rest his soul, I'll never forget his laughter and the joy of it rolling over the farmlands that evening as he slapped his knees, crying, "Sam! Sammy, my boy! Did you ever? Ever?"

The Age of Innocence had returned.

THE MASTERS
A Tale of Japan

IN THE MAIN CLASSROOM of an intermediate school in the prefecture of Shimane, Shigeru the Dunce was immersed in the twilight world of a reverie. Sunk in unfamiliar waters, he was gliding along the bewildering weedbeds of *sensei*★ Akamuro's latest lecture on Japanese literature and wondering how this new and confusing aspect of letters could be reconciled to fish and fishing.

Easily the tallest and oldest member of his class, Shigeru was acutely aware of the disparity in age and stature between his classmates and himself and at times it had made him uneasy. But more disturbing was the fact that his equally conspicuous inability to grasp the most elementary facts of Japanese literature was an obstacle to the realization of *sensei* Akamuro's hopes for an award in the yearly national scholarship contest.

Putting aside his nagging sense of inadequacy, Shigeru looked out the tall window and wondered how that particular day was affecting the fish and the insects of the waters well beyond sight but not of his imagination, where the stream beckoned with a magical voice, promising a fulfillment far removed from dreary grammatical exercises and purposeless equations.

★Japanese for Master

33

A voice cut through his reverie, a voice which until then had been the murmur of a distant waterfall. It was interrupted by the sound of his name.

"Shigeru Ito!"

Shigeru slid out from his desk and stood up, towering above his classmates.

"Sir?" His voice seemed incongruous with his stature. It was low and gentle.

"Will the honorable student Ito affirm the main points of my recent lecture on the influence of *The Tale of Genji* upon the literature of Japan?"

Shigeru's remoteness deepened to vacuity. He shifted his weight from side to side and shuffled his feet. Akamuro resumed, brusquely.

"Can it be that you have not retained one fact from the many I have touched upon?" Akamuro heard a low murmur.

"Please speak intelligibly!"

Shigeru took a deep breath and plunged in head first.

"The Tale of Genji," he began. *"The Tale of Genji . . ."*

"Thank you! The title is familiar to me! Go on!" A wave of tittering swept over the room.

"Go on! Say something!"

"Well, yes, *sensei. The Tale of Genji* is an important part of our Japanese literature. It is like Fuji—like a monument."

"Splendid!" cried Akamuro, striking the desk with the palm of his hand. "You can go back to sleep." The tittering rose again and fell. Akamuro now directed himself to the class.

"Listen to me carefully, all of you!" he announced. "I have decided to try an experiment. Instead of your usual homework I am assigning to each of you a paper on any subject of your choice. Mind, it is not to be a mere one- or two-page affair, but something broad in scope and which is of special interest to you. These papers are to be turned in to me one week from today." With this, *sensei* Akamuro dismissed the class for the day.

On the morning the papers were due the students filed toward the *sensei's* desk, each setting his respective paper on the growing pile. One of the last to come forward was Shigeru. Akamuro saw the thickness of the sheaf Shigeru had brought and began to speculate on what sort of grotesquerie the dunce had put together. He could not imagine what this young ass could conceivably have written about at such length. Or was it some kind of retarded joke?

Later, at home that evening, he began reading the class papers, saving Shigeru's for last. But, as the night dragged on, curiosity, which had been nibbling at him, finally had its way and he took Shigeru's bundle from the pile.

On turning the first leaf he noted the title written in a scrupulous hand: *Some Freshwater Fishes of Japan.* He began to read the first page and scarcely got midway when a curious thing happened. Akamuro's expectations of an illiterate, disorderly hodgepodge began to undergo an extraordinary change, first to interest then, as he read on, to wonder as he passed from Shigeru's introduction to the main text. Amazed, he saw the sureness with which Shigeru had described the first fish and the enthusiasm underlying his authority in describing its mode of life in its habitat and he could not repress the thought that here was a work of scholarship, perhaps a bit provincial, but nonetheless the product of a keen, observant mind. The paper went on:

"Of all our freshwater fishes, the trout is unique, not only in its beauty of form and grace and quickness of movement, but that its habit of feeding on nymphs and adult flies in both underwater and mature stages makes it an object of sport of the highest order, requiring the use of well-made and very resilient rods of the finest split bamboo, special lines, and artificial flies in imitation of the underwater or floating flies of the differing stages of fly development.

"Fly fishing is a sport demanding not so much patience and modes of baiting as for the coarse fishes, but of extreme caution and deliberateness of approach owing to the trout's constant alertness and keenness of vision. This constant vigilance makes it difficult to approach the haunt of the fish. For this and other reasons the trout is held in the highest regard by anglers as a prize. If not as large as other fishes, its capture is regarded as proof of superior angling skill."

After having finished Shigeru's treatise, Akamuro crossed from his study into the living room immersed in thought. His wife was sitting by a lamp, knitting.

"Hideko," he said to her. "This day I have learned an important lesson." She heard the gravity in his voice.

"Something unusual, evidently," she said.

"Unusual is scarcely the word," he said. "It is simply astonishing!" She stopped knitting and looked up.

"Was it something unpleasant?"

"No," he said. "Just bewildering."

"What happened?"

"As you know," he went on, "there is this overgrown boy, Shigeru, who scarcely ever listens to what I say, and spends most of his time looking out the window. He is still a full grade behind the others with little hope of ever catching up. He is not so bad at language and responds quite well to natural history. But from this point on his ears clog up so that barely a trickle gets to his brain. The other instructors tell me that the simplest problems in mathematics are utterly incomprehensible to him. And as far as history, there is little to be done. I've had to conclude that he is a hopeless dunce."

Akamuro lit a cigarette and went on. "Then without warning, like a shaft of sunlight from an overcast sky . . ."

Hideko had suspended her knitting and was listening attentively. Akamuro resumed.

"Last week I decided on an assignment unlike anything in the past. Why not? I thought. Let them have their heads. Something interesting might come of it. I asked them to prepare a paper on any subject of their choice.

"Did I say, surprising? Listen to this: I received a paper—no, really a small booklet—from Shigeru the Dunce, a text on the freshwater fishes of Japan done with such scrupulous attention to accuracy and detail that, well, I'm flabbergasted."

Hideko smiled. "That is truly remarkable," she said. "I can understand how you feel. It is like the stories of ugly frogs turning into princes and princesses."

"The astonishing thing," went on Akamuro, "is that he never gave any indication of this passion of his. It helps to explain his lack of response in the class, replying in monosyllables or, at times, with a blank look. His mind was focused somewhere else outside the window, sitting there, a full head taller, abstracted by other thoughts. . . . It may also explain his absences—truancies, pure and simple. He had run off from school to Nature's great classroom, following his own inclinations, pursuing his own studies."

"I see what you mean," nodded Hideko. "Shigeru's private world. He must have felt the great difference between it and the foreign nature—perhaps the artificiality—of your classroom. And the difference was so great he was compelled to conceal it under what you thought was his stupidity."

Akamuro was musing, his head moving from side to side. "Incredible! I should not be surprised if Shigeru were to find a post in the National Department of Fisheries—at the age of sixteen," he concluded, ruefully.

On the following day, as the time for dismissal approached, Akamuro asked in a kindly voice whether Shigeru would mind staying on a few minutes after school. Shigeru nodded, paying no attention to the scattered tittering of his classmates.

When the students had departed, Akamuro asked Shigeru to come forward. Shigeru stood before the master's desk speculating on what sort of rebuke he was to hear now.

"Shigeru," began Akamuro. "Your paper on the freshwater fishes of Japan is one of the best, if not the best I have ever received." Shigeru shuffled and lifted an eyebrow incredulously.

"In fact," Akamuro went on, "your description of fishing for trout with artificial flies is so fascinating as to make me wonder whether I might accompany you on one of your fishing excursions." Shigeru remained silent a while then, with a nod, replied, "I would be honored, *sensei*."

"Is the stream far from here?"

"There are many streams," said Shigeru. "One of the best is a distance off. I go there on my bicycle."

"Perhaps," said Akamuro, "it might be easier for the two of us to go in my car."

Shigeru nodded again. "By car," he said, "it would take only half an hour." The older man nodded with satisfaction. "What should I bring?" he asked.

Shigeru reflected a moment. His reply was measured and sober. "For the first time," he said, "it would be better that you watch me fish. Later on, you can begin to fish, little by little."

"I see," nodded Akamuro. "You mean that fly fishing requires experience?"

"Yes. And a lot of practice on dry land before you try it on the water."

"Would you teach me how to cast?"

"Yes, of course *sensei,* but first you'd have to learn how to catch simpler fishes. Trout would come much later; and you'd have to get the right equipment."

"Are fly rods expensive?"

"Yes. The good ones are made from the best cane by masters. And the best are very expensive. Mine cost me all my savings from two years of guiding."

"Guiding?"

"Yes. I have been a guide since I was twelve."

Akamuro shook his head in disbelief. "Extraordinary," he said. "Simply incredible. And who are your clients?"

"Business and professional people from different places. One doctor used to come from Tokyo."

"When do you think we can go?"

"Any weekend you like."

"Are you busy this coming weekend? I wouldn't want to interfere in your professional duties."

"I am free this weekend."

"Very good. I'll pick you up in my car. At what time should I be at your house?"

"At four o'clock on Sunday morning. Saturday I have some work to do for my mother."

"Isn't that a bit early?"

"No. After we stop the car we have to walk for another half hour."

On the following Sunday morning Shigeru led the way up a smallish mountain over a path which was barely discernible in the predawn twilight. Slowing occasionally in deference to his older companion, Shigeru stopped, noting with regret that *sensei* was wearing a white shirt. *If the trout catch a glimpse of that white shirt,* he thought, *they will scatter for cover. I should have told* sensei *to wear darker clothes. Now I will have to find a way to conceal him or keep him at some distance, else good-bye to this trip.*

A shift in the breeze brought the sound of surging water. "We are near to a small waterfall," said Shigeru. "We will go above it and fish a long run that is not so fast, so that you can see what is happening. However, you must not stay too close to me or the trout may see your white shirt. I should have told you to wear something less visible."

"I am sorry," said Akamuro. "I did not know."

As they came out of the woodland and approached the near bank, Shigeru turned to whisper, "Now try to keep a bush or a big rock between you and me. You can stick your head out and look." Akamuro tried to shrink as much as he could, the meanwhile quivering with excitement.

Shigeru had crept as close to the bank as he dared. Crouching, he knelt on one knee and began to swing his rod with short, rapid strokes. By degrees the line began lengthening as it looped back and forth in the air. Shigeru called in a low, soft voice, "*Sensei,* did you see that little ringlet there toward the middle of the stream? There! Again! Did you see it now?"

Akamuro hissed, "Yes, I believe I saw it!"

"That is a trout," said Shigeru. "He is rising to insects. Watch! I will place the fly a little to one side of the ringlet."

The line descended gracefully. The nearly invisible leader straightened and the fly alighted on the water like a colored puff of thistledown. The fly floated downstream without incident for some twenty feet. Now Shigeru deftly raised the rod, picked up the line, flicked it upward and began to lengthen it again. By now Akamuro was nearly beside himself with curiosity and excitement. He saw the fly alighting again. It had scarcely begun its float when the water under it shuddered, the rod was lifted smartly and now Shigeru was on his feet holding the quivering arch of the rod quite high as the trout zigzagged frantically toward one bank and the other.

Virtually spellbound, Akamuro had unknowingly left his hiding place and was standing at the edge of the bank. He heard the screech of Shigeru's reel as the trout bolted upstream and was looking on, his eyes wide, transfixed by the upstream drama. Shigeru checked the run of the fish and now Akamuro saw the rod tip plunging downward as the trout began to bore into a deeper part of the run.

Aware of the strength of the plunging fish, Shigeru knew that this was an uncommonly large fish for this stream and strong enough to rip the fly from the fine tippet. Skillfully averting disaster, he began yielding short lengths of line and was preparing for the trout's next move when he heard an enormous splash downstream. He turned and saw a white torso and two white arms thrashing frantically in the water. He dropped his rod carefully on the grass and dashed downstream. Floundering wildly and swinging his arms, Akamuro was trying to swim and gasping for air.

Shigeru slipped into the stream, took Akamuro by his shirt collar and began to yell: "Stand up! Stand up!" Akamuro was desperately swimming for his life. "Stand up! Stand up, you ass! It is not deep! Stand up!" The message finally penetrated and Akamuro stood up. "Come ashore," commanded Shigeru, leading the way. He called again from the bank and held out his hand. Strangely, Akamuro was groping ineffectually. Something was amiss. Then Shigeru saw that *sensei* had lost his glasses.

Entering the water again, Shigeru took him by the hand, led him ashore and told him to wait. "Don't move," said Shigeru, taking off his clothes. Nude, Shigeru entered the water and dived. He stayed under for some time, came up and dived again, this time a few feet downstream. When he surfaced again it was with Akamuro's spectacles in one hand. He waded ashore, put the spectacles on Akamuro's nose and asked, "Now, can you see?" Akamuro nodded solemnly.

"Thank you, Shigeru. I was careless. You see, I was carried away by the way you took that trout and . . ."

Shigeru dashed upstream along the bank, found his rod, and raised it. The rod tip bent again. The trout was still on! But this time it was not long before Shigeru led the trout in and beached it. He walked slowly toward Akamuro, who was sitting in wet clothes and wilted collar, and held up the trout. Akamuro shook his head and smiled.

"It is one of the most beautiful things I've ever seen!"

"Yes," said Shigeru, putting on his clothes, "and now let us go to our homes. You will want some dry clothes."

When Akamuro walked into his house later, a handsome trout dangling from one hand, his wife looked at him curiously.

"Your clothes look damp and wilted," she said. "Did it rain where you were?"

"No." He shook his head. "I was having a lesson."

"In what? In swimming with your clothes on?"

"In a way . . . Well, not exactly."

"And where did you get that beautiful fish?"

"My master caught it."

Hideko smiled. Akamuro chuckled rather wistfully. "I have learned something new."

"Yes?"

"Yes."

At the close of the following school week, Akamuro asked Shigeru whether he would stay on briefly after school. This time it was in a tone that was not a veiled command; indeed, the class had sensed a touch of deference in it. There was no tittering among the departing students. To the contrary, they had not quite got over their astonishment over *sensei's* praise of Shigeru's paper.

Freed now of any apprehensions, Shigeru walked forward and stood before the master's desk. After some hemming and hawing, Akamuro cleared his throat and began, obliquely.

"You know, Shigeru, I have been thinking a great deal on this fishing matter, and I must say that the thought of how the water, so innocent at the surface, can be charged with so much mystery, causing excitement at what may be underneath—it has captivated me. Who knows? I think . . . a small, bright fish, a medium-sized but wise fish—a *large,* fierce . . ." His arms were raised, the palms of his hands retreating until his arms were extended at full length. ". . . Ah! I now dream of fish—fish of all sizes, of many colors—Tug! Tug! Tugging at my line! But most of all I dream of trout—of one such as you caught with such great skill. Ah, er, Shigeru, would it, possibly . . . might we . . . perhaps . . . is it possible that I could learn, perhaps, to cast a line with a fly?"

Shigeru's reply was long in coming. He began to shift his weight from one foot to the other. He looked off in one direction and another and finally he remained still, his eyes fixed on Akamuro's necktie.

"It is too soon, *sensei,*" he began. "Too soon to think of trout. Fishing for trout is like higher mathematics. It takes much study, practice, and experience. We will begin with the addition and subtraction of small numbers, with the construction of simple sentences with simple words. We will begin with the little fish of the small pond, with the baited hook and the bobber, seated firmly, of course, on a bank that is not too high . . ."

"Ah," sighed Akamuro. "Then, you will take me fishing again—for a small fish—in a safe little pond?"

"Yes," said Shigeru, greatly relieved. "I will take you fishing again. You will proceed from one method to another, and then . . ."

Shigeru smiled. "When you have graduated, you will be ready to start on your post-graduate work in the art of fly fishing for trout."

Akamuro was already dreaming of the day. He nodded gratefully.

"Shigeru," he said, "you are a kind and wise *sensei.*"

A PHOENIX FOR DAN

PHOENIX: Mythical, beautiful bird which, every 500 years, consumed itself in fire, rising up from its ashes to new life.

NO ANGLER WORTH his rod will be surprised at hearing that Dan's story was delivered, as it were, on the bank of a river; nor, that the campfire had a hand in it. It would have had to, as we shall see. Besides, where there is a campfire there is always a story; and sometimes, as in our case, an Equation,* too. Moreover, it was a great fire—the sort that brings frantic calls to the forest ranger's telephone by an alarmed countryside.

The cause for this offense against the rules of responsible camping was old Dan Brenan, who made fly rods in the city, had been a camper much of his life, was an Adirondack historian, and should have known better, and who did know better, but whose spirit was irreconcilable to small fires when he was out of doors. And indoors, too, according to his patient wife, who had had to call the community firemen on more than one occasion when the flames in the fireplace had spread to the walls.

I suppose that this touch of pyromania may have been called a "quirk of character" by tolerant neighbors; but it would have been superficial, misleading, even demeaning. As it now appears in retrospect, a deeper meaning can be ascribed to the

---

*The now famous Equation establishing the quantitative Table of Variants in the relationship of Mass to Maneuverability—that is, in a fish. (See: *The New Mathematics,* Veritas Series, University of Bologna (NY) Press, 1949)

passion which, at evening, transformed that gentle craftsman and historian into nothing less than a ruthless Pharaoh commanding his slaves, the younger of us, to haul small trees to the site of his Pyramid; and never a glimmer of compassion for our hanging tongues and perspiring bodies. This, after having waded, literally, a mile of river, making innumerable casts under a broiling sun.

I think that, for Dan, the fire was the emblem of a soaring Spirit. Well back in his mind there may have been a nagging ambition to conjure up a phoenix of his own. If improbable, I must say in Dan's defense that the possibility of a phoenix sneaking out of an uncorked whiskey bottle into the fire, and soaring out its flames, is surely stronger on the banks of a river than anywhere else.

By this time I had become familiar with the rather unique pattern of Dan's camping. But at first one thing had puzzled me: Dan, a most knowledgeable angler, whose lore was well nigh endless, did not fish. After the tents had got erected and all was shipshape, Dan would solemnly take his favorite rod, a powerful, glossy black eight-and-a-half footer out of its tube, join its two parts meticulously, and fit it out complete with reel and leader. Then he would carefully lean "Black Maria" against a nearby limb, and there it would remain the entire weekend.

On this occasion, as the night advanced and Dan's fire "arrived," as it were, I finally asked the question I had suppressed so long.

"Dan, you don't seem to fish much, do you?"

The firelight seemed to emphasize Dan's resemblance to the farmer in Grant Wood's famous painting, *American Gothic*: the long, austerely set features, grim, expressionless, his wife and the pitchfork between them all of a piece out of a Puritan forge.

"I don't," said Dan. "And I do."

He meant, I thought, that it was enough for him to see us younger men go into the river. But a thought kept insisting that something had made him stop, had made it impossible for him to take Black Maria to the stream. Bill, the youngest of us, must have been thinking along the same lines.

"Dan, when was the last time you fished?"

Dan sipped his whiskey and began.

"On a river even bigger than this one, in another part of the country—it's a good while back, I suppose, as calendars go—but that day and that stretch of river are as vivid as if it were yesterday . . ."

A gleam of reflected fire from one of Black Maria's facets twinkled in the darkness as if the river-water of that memorable day had not yet dried. Dan continued.

"This river was known among us for the size and savagery of its trout, both rainbows and browns. It was, and perhaps still is, one of the most unique streams in the entire country because, regardless of its size, the trout, even the largest, would take a fly, and, happily for some of us, even a dry fly.

"I had decided to fish a reach of this river that had become famous on two counts. Just two pools above the one I selected, that great angling clergyman, Henry Van Dyke, had taken a seven-pound brown trout on a dry fly. The other concerned another, even greater trout, which had by now become a legend. He had broken many a startled fly fisher on a beat that extended well over a mile of river; and on more than one occasion, the savagery of his strike and the overwhelming strength and swiftness of the plunges that followed splintered the rods of men who, however experienced, had never known anything like it, and were left pretty badly shaken.

"By now this trout had been named Ulysses, because, like his ancient namesake, he was apt to turn up anywhere. Unlike other big trout, he was not content with being the boss of one or two of those huge pools. He was like a baron who considered the entire river as his domain. And that it was.

"It was a strange day, overcast, a day in which a fine drizzle seemed to be just barely suspended, falling sporadically and so imperceptibly as to keep me in perpetual doubt as to whether it was actually drizzling or not.

"Now, such overcast days, as you must know, are often productive, even though the scene is not as idyllic as one would wish.

"I waded slowly and very carefully out to a position that would permit me to cast my fly into the current so that, instead of inviting a dragging fly with the usual consequences, I should manage to bring off a number of good drifts.

"As I was settling myself I noticed a tiny whirlpool in the quiet water to one side of the edge of the current. I don't recall flies in any number in the air at the time, and so I was not too hopeful of interesting this fish with a dry fly, which, as you all know, is the only method that interests me.

"It was the time of the year which is probably the richest for trout in point of variety, size, and number of hatching flies: the Grey Fox was still showing, the Light Cahills had been coming in droves, the Dun Variant and Cream Variant were prevalent, as were any number of smaller mayflies and caddis, some peculiar to this river. Hoping it might be an inspired guess, I selected a large, number ten Multicolored Variant and tied it carefully to a leader point that was none too fine—actually a good bit coarser than usual.

"As I lengthened my false casts the little whirlpool appeared again. Aware now of a certain rhythm in that trout's feeding, I kept false casting to one side until it seemed about right to present the fly. It landed gently, a little to the side in the quieter water, and as it went by him, the fly, for some reason, did a pretty, slightly flirtatious little turn. As it did so, the water bulged, the fly disappeared, and I struck smartly, doing so against a force as unyielding as a log.

"The pool at that point was very deep, owing, I suppose, to the extensive watershed of that river and the powerful gouging of spring floods. The leader sank slowly out of sight, followed by a surprising footage of the line itself: the sinking movement stopped, leaving the arched and quivering rod and tense line pointing to the inert force beneath.

"As I began to recover from my astonishment I realized that this trout—if, indeed, it was a trout—was sulking at the bottom like salmon often do, and it occurred to me to try a device used by salmon men for stirring up a sulking fish. I began tapping on the butt of the rod. It took a fair number of strong taps and, sure enough, I saw that the tension was easing on the rod. As the fish rose he began circling to my right in the quiet water and began to head downstream.

"As the line passed me, cutting the water with slow majesty, I caught a glimpse of a huge shadow going by. Now, I may have reacted in some way and the fish must have seen me because he made a sudden lunge and began to swim downstream, gathering speed. The end of the line now flicked through the guides and the backing began streaking out, dwindling ominously on the reel, which was screeching away like a pack of hysterical bluejays. At once, a hundred or so yards below, the current unfolded, the huge form of the fish broke water, fell with a sickening splash and plunged on.

"For a moment I dared to hope that some quirk or, perhaps, its homing instinct would prompt the fish to turn upstream or into the slack water, but—and I knew it now—this was Ulysses, who, for all I knew, might be heading for the ocean."

At this point Dan's throat must have felt pretty dry because he stopped to take two sips of whiskey. Then he went on.

"Now, as I saw the backing melt away, I thought, 'Danny Boy, here is where we get off the train.' There was a sudden jolt, the line went taut as a fiddle-string for a split second and fell limp on the water."

It was a solemn moment for all of us listening there, one that called for a general sip, in salutation and mourning at once. But the story had not yet been told.

"Apparently," said Dan, "when he got to the end of the backing, the resistance at the breaking of the leader must have set the hook deeper and maybe hit a nerve or something. Stupefied, holding the inert rod trailing some two hundred yards of limp line and backing, I saw Ulysses jump clear of the water some three times, going even faster, if you can imagine it—and when he got to where the river turned sharply south he was going so fast that he didn't—he couldn't—"

"Dan! You mean . . ."

"Yes." Dan nodded solemnly.

"Good Lord, Dan! You mean he couldn't—make the curve?"

In those days the world was as young as the fledgling fly fishers sitting about the campfire we had erected for Dan. Now, even the crackling of the flames had submitted to the persuasive drone bass of the patriarch's voice. In the distance, well beyond the campfire circle, I could hear that great fish flopping heavily on that distant, gravelly beach, his powerful tail thrashing helplessly against the useless air. Or was it actually the current in the dark river below slapping against a boulder?

"Dan, did you go after him?"

"Well," said Dan, "it had all happened so quick that when I saw him down there, flopping like a frenzied seal, nothing much registered for a while. As I came to and began thinking about it he'd made his way back into the water. I can still see the waves he made as he tore into the shallows; and that big dorsal—like a flag, as he sank out of sight."

The fire had now settled, barely flickering over the glowing coals, when from its very middle there came a sudden upsurge of flame, followed by a puff of smoke that spread and soared towards the stars. In the silence I marveled. Could it have been Dan's phoenix, after all? Who knows?

ONCE IN A BLUE DUN MOON

I am sitting here, a sexagenarian immersed in wonder; wonder and disbelief. Today still another tackle catalog came in the mail. It was the fourth to offer capes of natural blue dun hackle. The fourth. Of natural dun! And these, too, were allegedly superb.

As I think on this glut, this obscene triumph of modern genetic science, wonder dissolves into irony. In my mind's eye I see an army of young amateur fly tyers complacently yanking hackle after hackle from scores—no hundreds—of blue dun capes, and I am about to weep. But I laugh instead; not just for myself, but for all of us of a time, not long gone, when natural dun hackles were as improbable, nearly, as hens' teeth.

Those were lean times; but no leaner than they'd been for centuries. And whoever aspired to the real thing eventually acquired the combined virtues of Jesus, Job, and Machiavelli. Even so, after having carefully charted your course, your voyage to one or another of the blue dun islands sometimes grounded on the reef of a breeder's agate-eyed indifference. You were prepared, of course, to deal generously, even sacrificially with the man; and you were so touched by your own goodness that you launched the first stage of your campaign on the waters of brotherly love. But as the day wore on you had sunk to the gravel and grit of attrition; and by nightfall you knew the futility of laying siege to a wooden Indian.

Long afterward you might learn that he hadn't heard you, because he was agonizing, too, but in a different way, over wounds throbbing in tender, private places, freshly bestowed that morning by Ye Olde English Blue Dun Game Cock with beak and spurs at fighting time.

With the passing of the years you learned to accept defeat as a condition of your search, normal as a pause for breath. By the time you had acquired a few dun capes—and by a few I mean two, or at most, three—certain facets of your mortality had got extinguished. You had become a master of subterfuge and camouflaged emotion; your passion had got stashed away in a remote internal cell where it still raged with unabated fury, but no longer betrayed.

As in other great quests your pursuit of Dun brought changes, some subtle, others not. Among the more telling of my own experience was the appearance of fantasies. Most were fairly chaotic, running a bit on the wild side. One, however, remained fairly rational and consistent, playing and replaying itself vividly, as it were, on an interior screen with full color and sound.

For the sake of others who have trudged the lonely deserts towards the mirage of Blue Dun and who will, understandably, be curious, I will try to give a literal version of it. And since it is, in a way, my own humble contribution to genetics, I feel I ought to introduce it with a short disquisition on racial memory, touching on the transmission of residual human characteristics.

But on second thought this might promote intellectual ferments with, as most fly fishers know, less happy results than with other kinds. So, on with the phantom chronicle:

THERE IS THIS Roman ancestor of mine, a cadaver of a man who, in an overlarge toga, is scarcely more than a bag of bones—a sort of odd fellow of few but sharp words who tags along with the legions on one expedition or another. He does not carry a sword. He doesn't believe in it. He rides a mild-mannered gray mare, and in his bags there are sheaves of papyrus and a number of reed pens for writing in them. A longish bundle of slender sticks protrudes from a fitted quiver. It is his fishing rod of three pieces.

When the battle is joined he sits to one side of the field and he writes. Afterward the centurions poke fun at him. "Fulvius," they say, "Look; we did it without thy brawn." Fulvius is dour. "This history," he says, "will record your victory. But you did not win. Nobody ever won a war; nor is ever likely to. You have merely sown the seeds of your own defeat later." Then he goes over to the prisoners and talks with them. More than historian, Fulvius is a scholar and a linguist, more interested in the customs, language, and dress of the barbarians than in how much land or livestock they have, or how much taxing they will bear for the revenue. But above all, Fulvius is fascinated by the natural beauty of their landscapes, especially the valleys where the brooks and the little rivers flow.

The prisoners are sullen. A few are cursing the Romans up and down: they, the generations that spawned them, their mothers, their gods. Fulvius agrees with them. "They are materialistic," he says. "In their passion for conquest they fail to appreciate the natural beauty of their new domains. For them, a stream is not the dreaming-place of the noble *trutta* but merely an excuse for building another bridge."

One of the Britons, a tall, lanky, fair-haired man, comes forward. "I saw thy saddle-quiver," he says. "It was not for to strike us down; and methinks thy writings of the battle will show impatience."

"Very likely they will," nods Fulvius, "for this very morning we did cross a gentle stream. On its limpid surfaces above the swaying reeds, there were dimples calling, sweeter to my eye than a maiden's kiss to my lips. It was to blaspheme my pen then, and these ambitious farmers in armor."

"Ah!" says the prisoner. "Those dimples were made by the *trutta,* as you call them. Many have I taken with the looping fly."

An extraordinary change comes over Fulvius's face. The clouds have drifted out of it, and the melancholy droop to his eyebrows has lifted. Under them is a beatific glow.

"Britannicus," he says, "now that this filthy business is over, they will take you back to Rome. But have no fear. Some well-born Roman wench will get you out of shackles. They are all the real bosses, I tell you. They'll not only free you, they will get you promoted. They adore fair-haired men. But in the meantime," he adds, "while we are here I would be grateful for you to show me this stream we were talking about. Then, your method intrigues me. Looping fly, you say? When we were in Macedonia I acquired a little skill in the use of the Astraeus fly, which was named after a great *trutta* river, and is made in simulation of a large fly of that water. Their fishers of the fly are men of skill and inventiveness. There is a sort of fellow-worker, a would-be historian by name Aelian, who has also remarked of this fly, saying they fasten red wool around a hook and fix to the wool two feathers that grow under a cock's wattles, and which are in color like wax. Clumsy, that, don't you think?"

"Quite," says Britannicus.

They have reached the periphery of the Roman camp and are halted by a guard. Fulvius raises his arm in salute and says, "Britannicus here is to be my guide." The soldier nods.

"You seem to have a lot of power," says Britannicus.

"That I have," says Fulvius, "and if it were Emperor Claudius himself, the story would be the same. They shake in their leggings at the thought of what I could do to them in my histories if I chose to. Now, about this Astraeus fly; do you use anything similar to it here?"

"No," says Britannicus. "Our *trutta* would laugh at such a gaudy body." Fulvius reflects a moment, then says, abruptly, "Excuse me, but I take it you must surely have a family name."

"Yes, of course," says Britannicus. "My full name is Algernon Cholmondeley Higginbotham-Smythe."

"A splendid name," says Fulvius. "Very sonorous; and may you live as long. But would you mind if I just called you Britannicus?"

"Not at all," replies the Briton.

"Which reminds me: How far is it to the stream?"

"A couple more miles. But on the way I would like to stop off and pick up my rod. Then, I think I ought to advise my wife that I'm still around. I must also fetch out a certain fly which I cannot do without. It is made with the hackle feather of the sacred cock."

"A sacred cock?"

"Yes. The rooster with the blue dun feather."

"Extraordinary," mutters Fulvius. "Simply extraordinary. Not that the color blue is unfamiliar to me. It is the dun part that puzzles me."

"Oh, that." Britannicus nods. "It puzzles everyone at first. And no wonder, because the color is neither blue nor dun, which is the color of a sooty sky before the storm."

"Then why is it called 'blue dun?' "

"Because it appears among the fowls but once in a blue dun moon."

"A blue dun moon?"

"In a manner of speaking amongst us."

"But, you say, neither the one or the other: yet it is called 'blue dun.' "

"It is only to give it a name, which is the way it looks when you first see it."

"You mean, it changes colors?"

"No. The colors are all there. It changes with the change of light. At times there is a touch of rust in it; or copper, gold, brass. Some would say that there is red in it, and tawny yellow, or honey, and quite capable, too, of bleeding a faint pink. There is then violet. Ah. Give me the day when it shows violet and that is the day when large trout glide up to it, as fat and casual as your Bacchus to a roast pheasant."

On the banks of the stream the day glides by and as Britannicus plies his fly among the dimples curling within the reflections of cloud and sky, Fulvius crouches nearby among the tall grasses. At last he has recaptured that high contentment grudged him by his profession. As the ritual wand weaves its spell over the men and the dimpling fish, he knows, as never before, the surge and retreat of subdued excitement playing within: the purest joy a man can know; the fly fisher at his trout. He studies his fair-haired friend's casting with keen intensity, the line uncoiling, straightening as the fly alights just to one side and above a dimple.

"By Jupiter, you have him!" cries Fulvius, *sotto voce,* as the great trout circles and plunges under the bent rod. He notes with admiration the skill of the Briton, as his arm yields momentarily to the trout's power, knowing that a false move will part the few horsehairs at the end of the braided line. Later, as the power of the fish begins to wane, Britannicus leads him gently toward the bank. Fulvius's hand reaches out with slow deliberation, and with a smooth, deft movement hooks his fingers into the trout's gill and lifts him out of the water.

"Well done, Fulvius!" cries Britannicus.

The sun emerges again from between the drifting clouds. In its glow a friendship ripens. It is Fulvius's turn. He looks at the hackle of the Blue Dun fly. It is violet. The gods are with him.

Nearly a year has gone by. Most of the Britannic legions have returned to Rome, and Fulvius has long since finished his account of the campaign. Weary of recording the exploits of these pompous farmers, he has, these last months, been haunting the poultry markets. Fulvius has by now formulated the hypothesis that there is not a trout stream in the entire known world whose trout will not respond to the Blue Dun fly; and this has led to the belief that it is a moral obligation—indeed, his duty as a historian—to test it on the Apennine streams to the north. That is, if he can now find a cock with a blue dun cape; for, as Britannicus once pointed out, there is no dye capable of transposing those varicolored glints to any other feather. They must be natural to the bird.

But in the night skies of Rome no blue dun moon appears. Fulvius dreams on and searches. Is it possible? That in all Rome there is not one? One noble bird carrying a glory of blue dun defiance on his proud neck? The weeks pass. Now his manner of staring into the market fowl-cages so borders on the grotesque that one Arab fowler is alarmed. "Move on," he says, "or I will call the *vigiles.*"

In moments of calmer reflection Fulvius inquires into the urgency of his search. Is it the feather's color? And the scarcity of these fowls? Or is it something beyond, whose elusiveness is so well exemplified in that color, color so mysterious among others so easily recognized and described? At last he decides to go find the Sybil and consult her.

At the temple, standing well to one side of the priestess, he casts the question gently, as if it were the fly of his dream color to the inscrutable.

"Priestess," he murmurs, "all honor to you, and my reverence. I would ask a question: Where is Blue Dun?"

The priestess bends over the smoking urn, inhales deeply of the acrid smoke. She sways and begins to moan:

> *Dun. Dun.*
> *The color of doubt.*
> *You'll find it deep*
> *In the eye of a trout.*

Fulvius bows respectfully and leaves, more bewildered than before.

It is June. Fulvius is wandering along the banks of the Tiber. There, under a brilliant sun, he sits listening to the birds and looking intently into the water. But no dimples appear on its surface, and no fly emerges. At last, with an air of resolution, he rises and sets off to go find Britannicus who, for some time now, has been installed in the great villa of Julian Verus, a general. Freed shortly after his arrival, Britannicus has been promoted twice. He is now the guard of the beautiful and virtuous Lady Livia's bedroom, which will foil any attempt on the part of anyone else to enter it and violate her honor while her husband is off to the wars. In the weeks remaining to Verus's return Livia's irritation increases day by day. Fulvius now surmises that when the general gets back he is going to have to promote Britannicus again, this time as emissary to Britannia; and in due time he may have a reasonably peaceful household again.

Fulvius enters the villa without so much as an announcement and bids a slave go fetch Britannicus. Shortly the slave returns followed by Britannicus, looking a little pale; and there are dark, bluish half-moons under his eyes. The two men embrace warmly.

"Britannicus," says Fulvius. "You look a bit tuckered out. You've been working too hard."

"Quite," says Britannicus, adding, "The job is very pleasant. Well, you might say, too much so. You know, sort of on your toes, and all that. It's a bit taxing. I really think I need to get away for a bit of a holiday—"

"That's what I came to talk to you about," interrupts Fulvius.

"There's a little stream north of here. It's one of those few that the Roman engineers haven't ruined yet. Moreover, no one fishes it; not even the natives."

Britannicus rallies. A gleam leaps to his eye. "Are you serious? Not even the natives?"

"Yes, there is a traditional taboo. It seems that a couple of desperate young lovers drowned themselves in it; and since then its trout are supposed to be sacred."

"But that would be worse than poaching. Sacrilege, you know. We might get killed."

"Remember," says Fulvius. "I am a historian. I could give them such a reputation that they would never live it down."

"But what about Lady Livia?"

"I'll take care of her, too. You just go out back and have the slaves get the chariot ready. See that you get the best horses. We don't want to waste any time. It's a long way over there to the Alba."

As he is leaving, Britannicus turns. "Which flies shall I bring? You know, I've never fished the streams of Italy."

"By all means the Blue Duns."

"Alas," sighs Britannicus. "I have but two left; one for you and one for me."

Fulvius is shaken. He grasps at a straw: "We will try to make do." But how his heart is heavy! It is a long way to the Alba. To lose that one Blue Dun fly—Ah! Tormenting images flit through his mind: A huge, ferocious trout surges up, engulfs that beautiful, innocent Blue Dun fly and rips it away. Forever. Then, even worse, the fly is snatched away high in midair by a swooping hawk; or—dismal day—trapped in flight by a predatory twig. . . . It is unthinkable.

That night a brilliant moon rises over the surrounding hills and soars in the Roman sky. As the night thickens a faint hue begins veiling the brightness, deepening imperceptibly into the small hours. In the hush before the first cock's waking a silvery blue dun moon is shedding a prophetic glow over the sleeping city.

But neither Fulvius nor Britannicus is aware of the prodigy in the night sky. Turning and tossing on their couches, they are dreaming of trout, waking fitfully, impatient for the first sign of light in the eastern sky.

In the half light of the Roman morning, as Aurora yawns and the first pale light appears in the eastern sky, a chariot turns furiously around a corner into the Way of the Northern Gate. As it hurtles under the great arch the guards, startled out of their dozing, see the chariot thundering off.

"It is Fulvius," says Annius, one of the guards, not very loudly. "I wonder at what mad histories he is pursuing today."

Annius is about to turn away from the receding cloud of dust on the plain when he sees something that provokes a grunt. Shading his eyes with one hand, he is looking intently.

"What is it?" asks Vitellus, his fellow guard.

"Have a look yourself," replies Annius. "Our distinguished citizens seem to have had an accident."

Vitellus fixes his eyes briefly upon the distant plain, then turns glumly to Annius.

"My eyes," he says, "they went bad after my last year's wine turned to vinegar. You tell me."

Annius obliges. "The dust is clearing," he says, "and it appears that they've collided with a chicken farmer on his way to market."

"Poor devil," says Vitellus. "It will cost him dear. For him it may be a disaster."

Annius grunts. "What a mess! And now what? Fulvius and Britannicus are running madly after one chicken. It's insane! If they really wanted to help that farmer, they'd gather up the nearby chickens."

"There was always something strange about Fulvius," says Vitellus.

"By Bacchus!"

"What now? Tell me!"

"They've caught the chicken!"

"And?"

"Fulvius is holding it aloft! Incredible! He's dancing with it! And Britannicus is dancing around him in circles!"

"Incredible!"

"Incredible? Hah! Much worse! They've been seized by a dementia. They are dangerous! They should be locked up!"

"I wonder," muses Vitellus.

"Wonder what?" snaps Annius.

"About that one chicken. Is it, maybe, some special kind of chicken?"

"There's nothing remarkable about chickens!" growls Annius. "They're good to eat, and that's about it! Except to offer as sacrifice now and then. Like that one," he adds. "He's a rooster; lean, sure to be stringy and unfit to eat. And he looks mean, like the kind they use for cock fighting. And what a color! It's unlike anything I've ever seen!"

"What about that color?" asks Vitellus.

"They've stopped dancing. Fulvius has taken some gold out of his purse-bag and given it to the farmer. And now it's the farmer who's dancing!"

Vitellus interrupts. "What about that color?"

"Oh, yes. The color? Well, it's a sort of grayish-bluish—copperish? Or should I say, bronzish? No. Wait! There are flecks of gold! By Bacchus!" A low laugh, strangely affectionate, nearly cooing escapes the old soldier. "It's beautiful! Can you imagine a deepening pinkish gold blue gray?"

Vitellus glances nervously at Annius and begins backing toward the stairway. He interrupts his headlong flight downwards to call upward, hastily: "I think my wife is calling me!"

Annius does not hear. As Vitellus gains the street he hears the sounds of distant whacking. It is Annius, slapping a thick, hairy leg, chortling:

"By Jupiter, Vitellus! I swear it's violet!"

SAINT THEODORE'S JACKET

ONE DAY NOT LONG AGO, when I'd begun to defer to the persuasions of age toward reminiscence, a small, frail man in a fringed buckskin jacket materialized at the bankside of a Catskill stream, plying a fly rod with quiet deliberation and care.

For some reason, not at all clear, I had the feeling he was familiar, or should have been, having been met, perhaps on occasions more meaningful than chance, at the edges of a sporting kinship.

This thought dissolved to a recall of places and events in regional histories. The Catskill Mountains then wore expansive mantles of stately, greenback hemlocks, trunks brooding somberly over its hidden roots. Bedded deeply below, these wove with spongelike intricacy, carrying drops of pure, cool waters threading their ways into descending basins and hollows toward the valley streams and rivers below.

Could it have been then that I met the little, stooped man with the fringed buckskin jacket and the big willow creel dangling at his side?

Memory's fingers riffled through the years and I was shortly aware that the likelihood of it was much too vague to have got stamped in memory. Indeed, how could it have done so? I was still a child living with parents in a city where the only streams that flowed visibly were the curbstone runoffs from sudden, heavy rains.

Nor could I have encountered him later on at the ponds of the surrounding farmlands. A boyhood destiny had mandated Sunday hikes from the end of the street-car line to the banks of one or another pond, carrying a short bait-casting rod, multi-plying reel, treble-hooked plugs for pickerel, and a small, col-lapsible stove for warming a tin of beans for myself and a young friend, a kindred Sunday truant similarly disposed, though not before having attended early Mass—a stern mater-nal command to be suffered interminably.

It was from Ross that I learned about Black Creek, some twelve miles from the city. In its dark, mysterious pools there lurked sinister-looking pickerel, also, but more importantly, smallmouth black bass.

Eschewing the timetables of bus transportation for reasons of empty pockets we soon became expert hitchhikers, relying on the generosity of motorists kindly disposed toward 15-year-old boys with telescoping fishing rods, trudging in hip boots, thumbs aloft.

From time to time we had seen bass rise to the surface to snatch an insect and concluded that flies would be more effec-tive than the ungainly, ominous plugs which made commotions disproportionate to small creeks. But fly rods were beyond our reach.

Then, one fine day when we were walking along one of the city's business districts I saw Ross bend down to pick up something he instantly thrust into his coat pocket. He motioned me to follow and ducked into a side alley. In the shadow of a warehouse Ross showed me why he always walked head down. He'd found a wallet. It was crammed with bills but bore no identification. He split the find evenly and the next day we went to a sporting goods store. Heeding the advice of a knowledgeable and helpful clerk, we bought fly rods, lines, reels, leaders, and large floating flies for bass. After a frenetic week of casting practice another Sunday came round. We returned from Black Creek with four legal-sized bass. Our careers as fly fishers had begun and bait casting became a thing of the past.

It was inevitable that sooner or later we should be drawn to trout. We were both avid readers of the outdoor magazines of the time, buying, borrowing, and trading them, gobbling up articles and stories about freshwater angling. The most appealing of them were of the quest for trout which swam elusively in storied streams, rivers, and lakes, evoking images of hikes through the dense forests of the Adirondack and Catskill mountains, fishing by canoe in the Canadian wilderness, making portages to hidden, unnamed lakes and ponds. A new world of possibilities with numberless destinations was opening up. An incredibly rich piscatorial life stood waiting in the mists of the future. But the realities of trout were to remain confined to an indifferent, large city and the warmish farmland streams and ponds accessible to us.

Meanwhile, as the years went by, the weekly violin lessons I'd been having for years had begun to yield results which were impressive enough to meet the standards which my teacher had set for me. I was the pride of my high school orchestra's director, a genial, competent conductor who discharged his duties with evident pleasure despite the intrusions of track and cross-country practice and inter-school competitive events. One year, having graduated, I decided to extend my ability as performer and was awarded a scholarship by a noted virtuoso then teaching at Syracuse University. I soon learned that my new professor was a passionate fly fisher. A cordial college and stream friendship ensued. Within driving distance many streams flowed, yielding trout of respectable size. During those years I met men who were dedicated fly fishers steeped in the tradition and lore of the American dry fly. At the end of this period I returned to the city of my birth and became a member of its philharmonic orchestra and two years later, of the Pittsburgh Symphony.

The need for finding some diversion from the pervasive ugliness of that city led me to the Carnegie Library which contained the largest collection of books on angling I'd ever seen. On one visit I pounced hungrily on a book on the life and writings of the patron saint of early American fly fishing. There, in a midstream photograph stood this little, thin, and somewhat stooped man with a fly rod, wearing a homburg felt hat, high starched collar, and tie, sporting a great, drooping handlebar moustache much too large for his delicate features. At his side stood a tall, handsome woman with an hourglass figure and an imposing hat of the period perched like a nesting stork on a generous hairdo. The man was the legendary Theodore Gordon, who had fled the confinements of a life of finance in New York City and an encroaching lung ailment to reconstitute his precarious health by tying unsurpassed flies for a small clientele, warming his numbed fingers over the feeble heat of a small stove during the savage, stultifying winters of Sullivan County in the southern Catskills. His female companion of the stream was never identified. After his mother she may have been one of the very few women to have ever brightened the life of that lonely reclusive genius.

Reflecting on Gordon's winters and the flickering little flame sustaining his dream of another spring to come, one must wonder at the spirit which sustains men, especially small, sickly men through the bone-chilling winters of the Catskills.

During that gloomy Pittsburgh winter I borrowed the book a number of times, always finding new discoveries and observations that transformed that puny figure into a colossus whose angling writings straddled an avid readership in England and the United States. Probing again into that photograph I tried to find some clue that might explain why Gordon had exchanged his fringed buckskin jacket for the bizarre and somewhat clownish formal attire. Finding none, I concluded that his fashionable companion had compelled him to honor her gallantry in wading alongside him ankle-deep in what were probably high-button shoes, by fitting himself out accordingly. Looking again, the great, drooping moustache began fetching images that were more mournful than suggestive of an abortive casting lesson intended for a festive day astream with a lady of high decree. That idyllic moment had been earned at considerable cost during the preceding winter.

There come days in the January Catskills when a pall the color of an inverted bed of old, sick oysters has overspread the frigid sky, and men have forgotten the sun if, indeed, it ever existed and, perhaps, never will again. This is the deserted time of the year when streams mutter funereally between icy lips, and glimpses of a near-forgotten youth appear in reluctant scraps of recall when a ray of pallid sunlight appears through a rift in the sky. The monotone whiteness of snow gives way to a flash of memory of a lush verdancy through which comes the sound of a current burbling hospitably. We rise, close the curtains on the nascent blizzard and turn inwardly, hoping the elusive episode of spring will remain a while, if only to impress on the numbed brain a vision of what may lie ahead—something the organism had not quite forgotten after all, and which another cycle will restore to us after having expiated the barren time of the year.

Should the sorcery of our hopes prevail we may be able to defer the hostility ahead and turn our thoughts toward summer streamsides and the friendship of anglers one has been privileged to know, and others less familiar, encountered in books and dreams.

It was this all-embracing thought that finally resolved the old insistence that I had encountered Gordon. Simply, at one time or another I had seen this photo of Gordon and his lady and it had remained quiescent in an obscure niche of memory.

One spring I resigned from the Pittsburgh Symphony with no regrets. I returned to the clean, pure environs of my Catskill Mountain village and the friendship of a coterie of fly fishers, amiable anglers all.

Among them was Roger, one of the most passionate, dedicated and perceptive fly fishers I'd ever known. One evening after a day's fishing on the upper Delaware I mentioned Theodore Gordon. Heads over dishes of cold *calamari* I'd cooked the day before, and glasses of white wine, Roger's usually calm features began to liven up. He was nodding vigorously. "Gordon?" he said, "that's the greatest name in American fly fishing. Ever read his notes and letters?"

"Yes," I replied, "much, perhaps all of it over the years. It's a monumental book—a mural which conveys Gordon's stature as a pioneer fly fisher, innovator—in short the fountainhead of modern American dry-fly fishing."

He reflected thoughtfully. "I've read it many times. Even today I came across something I'd somehow skipped or hadn't really digested. I'll be forever grateful to John McDonald for having written it and to Nick Lyons for having published it." He waved a tentacle on the end of his fork. "That little runt of a man's writings are as fresh today as when he first wrote about fly fishing, fly tying, and American stream lore. Notwithstanding all the hoopla and bullshit by later writers who were scrambling for reputations, he was, and is, the Master."

As the night advanced, Roger began elaborating on his own quest for a personal link to Gordon's great tradition and of his regrets at having missed it in his lifetime. Then, in a memorable transition he modulated to gratitude for having come to it as close as he had by pursuing his ideal at second hand, seeking out Gordon's former friends, now quite old but still active and lucid. Roger continued, "I went to look up

Herman Christian. Now in his mid-eighties, he had chopped down a bee-tree which had annoyed his young wife a long time. Then we went in and got into his cider barrel. He got real lively and began to talk of Gordon as if he'd passed away the night before."

"Herman wasn't exactly a blushing violet about his own ability as a fly fisher, and began flaunting his conviction that of all Gordon's would-be friends he'd outfished them all, Gordon excepted, because, he said, Gordon was as secretive about his catches as of his fly tying, for fear of giving away his secrets. Few, if any, had been permitted to watch him tying flies. You had to be content with seeing the finished article, noting the artistry of his tying, not to mention the many innovations he'd brought to the American angling scene."

I was to learn that as a very young man, Roger had been a charter member of *The Theodore Gordon Fly Fishers,* a society in New York City. He later withdrew to extend Gordon's affiliates far from that city to the burgeoning fraternity of fellow anglers of the hill and valley streams of the Catskills.

That Gordon's spirit had got transmigrated somehow, to my friend, Roger, was not merely a conjecture arrived at by my experience of this remarkable companion of mine, but a palpable reality documented by many days astream and a pervasive respect for a mysterious, compelling belief that this model angler had, by some mystical means, inherited Gordon's mantle. This was borne out in a revelatory event when, one day at his home, Roger opened a large trunk, and after some rummaging held up a fringed buckskin jacket.

"Years ago," he said, "the *Fly Fishers* raffled off what was left of Gordon's estate. I drew a lucky number somehow, and here it is, the Prince's own fishing jacket. They say it was big for him, and it's a bit small for me; but I never fail to wear it once a year at mid-season. The Quill Gordon fly may have long run its course, but for me that's Saint Theodore's Day."

THOUGHTS ON FLY FISHING

ON HAVING TURNED his seventy-fifth year in reasonably good health any fly fisher must feel an immense gratitude to the Great Spirit for having been granted the privilege of rivers and streams over the years.

Acknowledging the precariousness of this stage of life, I begin speculating upon how much longer my legs will carry me astream before having to put the rods away for the last time. Images flit by recalling those remarkable men who, at ninety, were still winging flies waist-deep in favorite pools. But I dare not tempt myself that far, lest I put a jinx on what the future may hold. I will look to one more season instead, while giving thanks for each new day.

In the meantime, as the huge old pine tree at the side of the house groans in protest against the chill blasts of Catskill December, a mood of reflection creeps into the day watches. But it wants to move on toward something closer to the life of the sport, of certain thoughts and feelings evoked along the way. Memories exclusively are only too suggestive of retirement to the strains of Bach's *Come Sweet Death*.

Given a fair lucidity and recall, this may be as good a time as any for reviewing a lifetime's experience of fly fishing, and may be preferable to a mid-life account in which the new enthusiasms can distract the angler from aspects of the sport more revealing of its totality and depth.

Many before me have sung of the blameless sport; but if I did not salute it in my own way I should be remiss in acknowledging my indebtedness to it, and accordingly, to the great bounties of Nature with which it is so closely interrelated.

It would be presumptuous of me to add my two cents' worth to the cumulus of angling literature but for the potential fly fishing still holds for experience, differing points of view, and the enormous appetite anglers have for reading and talking about fishing. As long as one angler remains, the last word will not have been said. And if anglers are not to be pleased equally, it may be for the same reason that each one believes or suspects that his experience is unique; and being little different, I ask no one's permission for getting on with mine.

I doubt whether any other recreational sport has so captured the imagination and secured the lifelong devotion of its practitioners than that of fishing for trout, salmon, and other fishes in free-running brooks, streams, rivers, and lakes with the artificial fly. In our country this community is formed by men from every walk of life whose sources of livelihood range from day labor to the most rarefied fields of intellectual inquiry, research, and the arts, and a surprising number of women of every age who perform their roles from housewifery into the professions, business, and the arts with inimitable aplomb. It would be reasonable to assume a wide variety of temperaments in anglers of both sexes with a fair potential for discord but for the power that transcends all their differences, and that is the sorcery of water.

Over the five centuries of recorded angling tradition many have written of their sport with affection, eloquence, and skill. Some of these writings are as pertinent today as when they were written. At their core there is inevitably a love of rivers great and small. It runs through them all like themes of musical works ranging from the solitary folk-songs of mountain rivulets to mighty symphonies.

The ancients took to the rivers for baptism. Our river-folk reverberate to that old and sensible theme of purification. In other than physical ways the river has the power to cleanse the soul of motivations gone awry in men disposed by nature and training to honesty. We turn to the rivers to recapture an innocence of heart and mind we knew at infancy.

It has been surmised that a love of rivers may be a manifestation of racial or tribal memory, which presupposes an ancestry at or near to flowing waters at some remote time in history. But the magic of flowing waters is felt so universally as to incline me toward a more immediate cause, one that might explain the response to rivers in those whose lineage winds in an unbroken chain through desert and semi-arid countries since Biblical times. Far more reasonable to me than vague groupings into the archives of Man is that period of our first sensations and stirrings before birth when, snug and warm within our mother's edifice, we first heard, as she slept, the pulse and murmur of the stream as it surged from the springs of her heart and went running its course through the arterial valleys of that world of our first wakings. A rather fragile supposition perhaps, but I doubt whether it is contestable. Indeed, our custom of referring to rivers and streams as feminine could be ascribed to that first experience.

From time to time I have been asked why men fish. The question is as foolish as asking why they breathe. This is not meant to accuse the uninformed of stupidity. Rather, it gives a notion of the gulf created between himself and others when a man becomes an angler. The nature of the sport compels an involvement so wholehearted as to create the impression that the angler at his sport is oblivious to anything else. This impression is not merely correct: it is an irrevocable fact. Whoever would attach blame must lay it to water.

For the few among the heathen who wish to pursue the matter, I should explain that fly fishing is not simply a diversion, a game, or a competition sport. It can be any or, at worst, all of these, but above all it is a passion. One may have heard of a certain person: He'd rather fish than eat. There are many like him. But even more remarkable are men who would rather fish than make love. However, most anglers I know have found a more satisfactory equation in taking the best of both worlds. It tends to lessen the risk of an uncertain marriage and results in children who may one day go staggering, rod in hand, around the river stones and fall in among the progeny of the fish and insects once visited by their father.

In a highly symbolic and dimensional way, angling is an expression of an eternal quest. In streams the fisher may find the same deceptive transparency as in himself and the same sense of mystery as the shallows fall away to unseen depths as the stream rolls onward towards the sea from which, at some remote eon, he first emerged.

There are some among us who say they go to the river only to catch fish; and to watch them one is inclined to believe them. But there is always something more to it than the fish. In the reminiscences of the coarsest fish-hog we can discern, if we care to, a remnant of sensibility which tells us that this animal is not as impervious to the song of the river as he sounds. Among them are those anglers in whom the grinding poverty of childhood and youth can never quite silence the clamorings of necessity. Far to another side are the few in whom evolving took place before birth. In them one may find an inherited sense of proportion and an awareness of the dangers of tampering with the delicate balance of Nature, leaving us the impression that they are born conservationist-anglers.

But most anglers occupy the wide area between the two extremes, the mid-catagory of devotees who acquire a deepening appreciation of the sport by frequenting streams at every opportunity and by reading and fireside fishing with fellow anglers. Let us go to the river with one of them.

His rod joined, his reel firmly fastened to its butt, he threads the line through the guides and stands immobile looking intently over the pool for a telltale sign or ringlet. From a small box he selects a fly and attaches it to the fine point of the long, tapering filament of deception. Then, ever so slowly, he enters the water.

As he stands against the uncertainties of the current, finding himself dwarfed by the forested contours of the mountains to each side of him, he sees how far above the mountain tops the sky is. At once he knows his place. True, his machines can take him far beyond the mountains. Yesterday he visited the moon, and tomorrow will find him circling a planet. But he will always be small in the eye of a river. The pride of earthlings which he shared yesterday has shrunk to lowliness as he makes his cautious way among the stones and boulders of the river; and this walk in wonder and modesty will touch him as the boldest stroke of astral navigation never can. He has entered the stream in gladness, for he knows that in yielding to its mood and tempo he will soon know release from his burden of artifice, and he knows, too, what and where he is in his heart. Aware now that he is a fair way to acquiring humility he has, in that instant, an intimation of a superior manhood, one that does not fear the consequences of humility. And when, on leaving the river, he re-enters the world of men, he brings a breath of the river to it. His world may not mark the event; but multiplied thousands of times by other anglers, the recurring little benedictions must work their persuasions like a soothing oil to the abrasions of mankind.

Fly fishing is almost invariably identified with the best that Nature has to offer. Following upon cataclysmic upheavals over eons of time, transitional improvisations have left to us the watercourses of the world as we know them today, a rich heritage so varied in character, size, and scope as to fulfill the dreams of the gentlest to the most adventuresome angler. There are the meadow streams of England, France, and Yugoslavia, flowing bank-full all year. Closely related in character are the spring creeks of eastern Pennsylvania that surge up in full flow from deep limestone beds. Their idyll of weeds swaying to the *sotto voce* murmur of crystalline water is retold by the spring creeks of the American West, challenging master fly fishers to the limits of skill against large and very finicky trout who think very highly of their skins.

More compelling to the bold are the huge, brawling rivers raging with elemental fury against the walls of deep, dark canyons and racing through the Alpine forests and meadows of the western states, or shouting out over Scandinavian valleys, calling on giants to try the mighty waters hurrying toward the fjords and the sea. The rivers of Alaska, New Zealand, and South America have come into their own in recent decades as heavens for living anglers. But in perhaps no other country in the world is the angler blessed with so varied and great a number of trout waters as in the United States.

The perpetual movement of the world's watercourses has witnessed countless histories of the ages of Man. That slice of water which glides by so innocently has gone to sea many times. How many? We are left to a feeble surmise of the scope of its metamorphoses.

At times I see nothing more than an elusive element through which the trout, unseen, are weaving, gliding up to a hatching dun or darting and plunging furiously among nymphs at the peak of the hatch. I see mostly what I am looking for: the dimple, the flouncing wavelets at the surface commenting on the underwater dance.

There have been days at the riverbank, not necessarily grey days, when a particular choreography in the current awakened a nostalgic memory for an old friend, long dead, whose ashes I strewed one melancholy June morning in the Beaverkill River. As they trickled from the canister they were enfolded by a portion of the flow which had arrived after ages of transposition at precisely that time.

Years afterward, at a passage of the current, the image of Fritz would glide across my mind's eye. Why so? He was an ordinary man. But in an important sense he was not. For reasons best known to the gods of fly fishing he had seen fit to befriend a younger companion whose shattered marriage and impoverished spirit were made bearable by cheering weekly trips to the river in Fritz's fishing car. Generous, kindly Fritz, it was you who affirmed my belief in the latent nobility of some seemingly ordinary men. This and other thoughts went unremarked by the water as it went its eternal way, accepting the ashes, returning years later by chance or design to pass before an aging man whose sight had begun to dim but whose inner vision had quickened toward some ultimate truths on the meaning of life.

Dangeau, a famous French wit, dining at the table of one of those early, unwashed monarchs, was asked by the king about all the reading he did.

"Sire," replied Dangeau, "reading does for my mind what your majesty's partridges do for my cheeks."

In a comparable way, fly fishing does for my soul what religion was supposed to do, but did not. Concluding long ago that I had been misled, even defrauded, I left all the denominational sects of Christianity and Judaism to hang each other in the names of their particular deities and took myself directly to God in Nature who acknowledges my presence by admitting me to the miracles of Creation.

Fly fishing lends a redemptive touch of the esthetic to the purely animal manifestation of Man's heritage of the pursuit and killing of fish and game for sustenance: the rod springing to life, the changing rhythms of the lengthening cast, the line looping tautly as in a mystical rite, the fly fluttering and descending on or under the surface—these all together seem to weave a magical spell to which the angler gladly submits. The delivery of the fly at or near a riseform conjures up an expectation which may be fulfilled at any time or not at all; and the expectation may not abate until after the very last cast at dusk when the rod has been disassembled and put away. Was the day wasted? In a purposeful way it was not; for the prolonged suspense will remain with him as an ungratified wish which will surely be granted on the next occasion. If only for this reason, the confirmed fly fisher seldom turns away from his sport, and if so, not for long. He knows that if he cannot accept an uneventful day he is not worthy to be called a fly fisher. I have known days astream when dry-fly fishing was little more than an ironical paraphrase of the Biblical dictum: "Cast thy bread (fly) upon the waters and it shall be returned an hundred fold."

By the time I was baptized as fly fisher, Theodore Gordon was already a legend. I think that his canonization was owing as much to his originality in devising specific patterns for American waters as for a certain nature that led this short, frail man to turn his back to success as a financier and embrace an "unrealistic" ideal that was calling to his spirit. For the privilege of four months' fishing in spring and summer, Gordon was willing to endure the bitter Catskill winters, creating new fly patterns, warmed partly by a small stove, partly by the replies from his correspondence with noted British anglers.

Gordon's studies of insect life led to the imitations that were pivotal in the revolution in fly design for American waters. I doubt whether Gordon would be particularly flattered by the gratitude of the fly fishers to follow, or moved by our admiration for his courage in forsaking all to follow the little prophet within. Simply, he had given his heart to the river in return for which the river gave of its essence, an essence that slowed the course of the fatal illness that was to take him prematurely to the eternal streams.

One of the surest things that can be said of fly fishing is that it is inconsistent. Unlike golf, in which the greens are well maintained and the players subjected only to the whims of weather and wind, the factors involved in fly fishing are much more diverse and complex. The stream is never quite the same on any two successive days. The water may be high or low, disposing the fish differently. And as compared with a golf ball, a trout is a living, alert, suspicious creature constantly adapting to the moods of the stream, requiring adaptation in the angler's method. While trout are capable of rising freely during feeding periods, at other times they can hold dourly in static indifference to anything the angler can offer.

This change of mood applies especially to American free-stone streams, contrasting sharply with the relatively well-bred chalkstreams of England and the spring creeks of the United States which flow with remarkable stability the entire year, thus reducing the uncertainty of the one great factor with which the freestone angler must contend.

It may be that a good part of the allure of fly fishing lies in its very incertitude: The perfect day, the near-perfect water conditions can and often do draw a blank. An overcast day with a fine drizzle may prove to be the best day of the year. One might say that the charm of angling lies in the imminence of surprise. The largest trout of the year taken on an otherwise dull, uneventful day is precisely the sort of thing that obliterates the memory of fishless days and reinstates the mystery firmly in the angler's hintermind.

Anglers who meet at the waterside do so on a sort of neutral ground, a little world apart whose spirit takes no notice of this or that man's weightiness in the balance of social and business eminence. Indeed, during this time at the river some strange harmonies are created in the sympathetic bond that may grow between two men whose ethics in professional life may be at variance. The angler who disapproves of parasitism will understand me when I remind him of the fly fisher he met at the stream last year: a perfect gentleman, generous in the exchange of flies, courteous in yielding the pool, and a charming companion at the bar later. How much we can forgive, the compromises one can make are best understood by an angler in the field whose sport, like the confessional, absolves nearly all sins except those of taking and keeping undersized trout, fishing with hardware, or urinating in the stream. That our admirable stream companion was later expelled from the American Stock Exchange for manipulations that may have brought ruin to innocent persons seemed somehow remote beside the memory of the near-perfect angler.

Two of the most amiable fly fishers I have ever met were Americans of Italian descent. Both were gentlemen of the angle; one in the traditional, the other in the American colloquial sense of the word. Both were deeply immersed in the sport. Later I learned that one was one of the subtlest and most relentless operatives of the Federal Bureau of Investigation. The other, surprisingly, proved to be a high-ranking chief of a notorious organization. I saw no difference in the quality of the flies they gave me nor in the cordiality of their company. But the experience effectually dispelled any lingering doubts as to the fate of Waltonian amiability and gentleness in some anglers in their off-stream pursuits.

In another piece I have written at some length about an obsession: my quest for the elusive natural blue dun hackle. In a more rational person the unfounded rumors, the false leads, the recurring failures would have been more than enough for a lifetime. But rationality—what little there was of it—was to be subverted again. I was stung by a sliver of bamboo, and when the infection set in I was on my way.

Three generations of rodmakers had evolved rods of differing character and "actions," each of which had qualities appealing to one or another angler, each with his own notion of what should be expected from a fly rod for differing streams and methods for varying conditions. Over the years I had heard a good deal of controversy among anglers about rods and their makers, much of it seldom voiced under a *mezzoforte,* and the reverberations of the din in my head became a settled clamor of speculation.

I had long ago acquired an 8-foot rod from its maker, Dan Brenan, for which I had given violin lessons to his daughter. It had been designed for dry-fly fishing and was resilient and powerful enough to have served me for a lifetime. But the hoarse creakings of fellow anglers had aroused me to feverish calculations over the virtues of rods by other makers of the classical American school and those of England and Scotland.

In due time I acquired rods by F. E. Thomas, Winston, E. C. Powell, Leonard, Orvis, Halstead, Garrison, Hardy, Pezon et Michel, Farlow, Howells, Kushner, Thomas and Thomas, and by that great and humble master, James Payne.

Confronted again by the thought that the Brenan rod together with one or two by other makers would have been quite enough, why then the perennial search? It could suggest a defect of character, or an insatiable possessiveness were it not that since my search ended some years ago I have kept four rods, an original Payne and three for light and intermediate lines by Payne's disciple and worthy successor, Walter Carpenter. All the other rods were traded or sold to dealers and other anglers, sometimes at a loss. I imagine that my experience of bamboo helped keep the circulatory system of rodmaker-dealer-angler relations in good working order. Would I now trade that experience for a reconstitution to my anemic bank account? Or for a certificate of sanity? I would not, for I should not have known myself nearly so well. Nor, I should add, would I trade one of my cane rods for any six allegedly advanced rods of synthetic materials, which make better sense for heavier lines for larger fish.

I have said that fly fishing is a passion. As such it can still be tolerated within the social and domestic frameworks. But when carried a step further into addiction its containment becomes uncertain. Wives and sweethearts of addicts may become uneasy over the prospects of dilution of relationships with the men of their choice; and in extreme cases they may sense a threat of dissolution. They are intuitively right. The stream is a woman.

As for anglers who are confirmed bachelors, the stream may be the only woman they ever knew or care to know. This need not reflect discredit on their manhoods. Many factors could have determined the choice: an unrequited love, fear of invasion of privacy, or simply an indisposition to a conjugal way of life. There are other factors, and few are necessarily condemnations of manhood. It is a quality rather than a quantity. Given certain crises, the great football star, the war hero may not prove to be half the man that the sickly looking Mister Nobody is in facing up to his duties and responsibilities. The matter is intensely personal; and it is a rare man indeed who, presuming to judge others by his own standard, does not risk being proven an ass in the long run.

At her summer's best the stream can be a beautiful, smiling wench, as enigmatic as ever, to be sure; but as you are drawn to the rite you have the feeling—or is it wish?—that she will probably yield up her favors on this day. And when at evening you meet a fellow angler with but one trout in his creel you are not to be misled by the pulling at your own shoulder strap into offering consolation, nor to show disbelief if he offers you his trout. It may well be that his heart's creel is overflowing, his sensibilities restored afresh by one of the sweetest days of his life.

Touching on the spirit of the sport should not diminish the importance of its technical and utilitarian elements. I know as well as the next angler that much of the pleasure of fly fishing consists in the excellence of our equipment and the confidence and ease of casting acquired by practice and experience. There is then so much more to it, embodying as it does a knowledge of the stream, the strategy of the approach, a substantial working familiarity with its natural flies in differing stages, the ability to meet some, if not all, situations, to present the fly in a lifelike manner, and then to play a trout to land or net with skill for keeping or releasing as the angler chooses.

Assuming that the foregoing and a good deal more are known to most anglers, I have chosen, rather, to write of attitudes and other phenomena which hover about the sport like an aureole. When perceived, they may help awaken the angler of modest experience to things which some of our fishing celebrities may never get to know much about. The professional angler caught up by the necessity to have to maintain his reputation is, in one sense at least, a sort of unlucky trout—one that is caught nearly every day of his life by the same irresistible fly of competition.

In our day of depletion—owing in part to the brilliant successes of our chemical corporations in securing permits from state and federal agencies for poisoning rivers and very large bodies of water—the angler of moderate skill who neither thinks like a trout nor casts like an accuracy champion had better learn to enjoy the amenities of the sport by reducing the importance of a catch until it has lost its potential for spoiling the day with anxiety. When we have accepted whatever the day has to offer, we have begun to live that day, for we have accepted Nature. In this renunciation of ambition to succeed, its attendant easement of tensions opens our eyes to the miracles of existence all about us which might otherwise be a negligible background to the taking of fish, which, for some constitutes "the real thing."

I have tried to explain anxiety to myself elsewhere as the state of being somewhere else than where one is at. But the fact which lies coiled in that simple statement belies its simplicity: for the tensions which occur as a result of the opposing pulls of the states of mind can bring on, at the least, psychic discomfort and at the extreme, a state of panic culminating in disturbances of the personality. But as a rule, the angler's occupational anxieties disappear the moment he enters the stream or shortly thereafter. The reason, as it appears to me, is that in some magical way, his quest at the stream compels him toward the immediate present. I doubt whether anyone is capable of feeling the present more intensely than the fly fisher unless it be a religious adept in the art of meditation. True, the angler may be excited by the prospect of a favorite riffle ahead, but not to the extent of squandering the reach before him. He knows, or should know from experience, that little may be taken for granted; and he may well find the best fish of the day where it was least expected.

Some anglers fish because it provides a respite from the hurly-burly of their lives. For others it is a disentanglement from the sticky fly-paper of social obligations. For a few a marginal existence depends upon the catch. And then there are those for whom it is a point of honor and sometimes necessity to poach on restricted waters, and who would be depressed by the prospect of having to fish in public waters. Such men are held to be outlaws. But I am inclined to think that the same spirit in the river draws them all alike, though its call is interpreted differently. The poacher moving stealthily at night along the river has his own poetry; and perhaps he hears things confided by the river which it will not divulge in the daytime to the sporting angler. They may not know it, these two, but it is only the difference of circumstance in their lives which has separated them and made them strangers and perhaps even enemies of each other. But however he may be regarded, let us not overlook our debt to the night fisher for ridding freestone streams of those great cannibal trout which slaughter the smaller fish at night and during the daylight hours look out from their shadowy lairs with scorn for the paltry offerings of fly fishers.

I have heard it said that fly fishing is an art. I agree, but only conditionally, and not with the popular connotation of artist to anyone who fishes with the artificial fly. The term may be applied only to those men and women whose approach to the sport reveals an integration of the qualities of dedication and attention to details which make up the "compleatness" without which art is unattainable.

A phenomenon of our time, with its preoccupation with advancing technologies, is that of men who would make a science of fly fishing. One professional in particular is a sort of marvel of scientific exactitude. He has, literally and figuratively, left no stone unturned in an effort to drag fly fishing into the mausoleum of exact science. The result is for me, as perhaps for others, appalling. I use this word advisedly in that, after having given the sport a lethal dose, he sets about replacing the original fluid with formaldehyde like the bright undertaker he is. I do not envy this man's highly publicized angling excursions around the world, and his ambition to catch and display more and larger fish than anyone else—an ambition, I might add, which has often been "cut down to size" by less arrogant and quite unscientific anglers. He has long forgotten—or fame may have prevented his ever knowing—that the trout, the salmon are not the only objects of our quest, but concomitants to the greater quest in the mysterious waters of our own selves.

To say that fly fishing can be an art is more appropriate— that is, if the sport can be categorized at all. While science aims at exactitude and empiric results, art in angling consists of a balanced interplay of the intuitive (subconscious) and rational (conscious) faculties. Since this takes place entirely within the angler himself, he is close to his innermost nature or, if you will, his soul, whose protection requires vigilance and care. Stated somewhat differently, the art of fly fishing may be attained by surrendering our egos to the stream. And when we have done so, we are likely to recapture innocence again, a catch beside which a cartful of trophy trout is insignificant.

This thought resurfaced one day. I was supposed to be practicing on my violin and should have been concentrating on the music when the thought did a sudden, deft turn. "All art," it began, "is angling." Astonished, I put the violin and bow away and sat at my desk. The pencil began scribbling away, elaborating:

"Since prehistoric times onward the artist has sought to expand the layman's life experience by admitting him through his senses into a new microcosm created from materials, color, musical sound, and the spoken and written word. One might say he interprets his own evocations, transforming them in accordance with a particular sense of order, in doing so giving the world of men an affirmation of its own potential for creativity.

"After having sifted his impressions of the exterior world, it remains for the artist to take them into his interior world, a mysterious element into which he must probe. It is at this point that the artist becomes an angler, an inveterate, dedicated angler whose life and works hang by the qualities of his evocation, intuition, and skill."

The effect of flowing water upon persons of sensibility and its capacity for tapping hidden psychic springs is felt universally among the peoples of the world in connotations less piscatorial than religious.

In her admirable anthology *The World of Zen,* Nancy Wilson Ross quotes Gensha, an old Zen master who, when asked how to enter the path of Buddhism, replied:

"Do you see that stream?"

"Why, yes."

"There," said Gensha, "is the way to enter."

Ms. Ross goes on to quote a haiku (traditional 17-syllable poem) by the poet Gochiku:

The long night
The sound of water
Says what I think.

In the older Roman Catholic ritual of the Mass the first words of the celebrant are: *Introibo ad altare Dei,* literally, "I approach the altar of God." There are anglers whose approach to the stream is scarcely less reverent; and in certain individuals we may discern something akin to awe, as on the brink of some impending mystery. Watching one such could raise the question: Has this man been distracted from the business of fishing? I don't think so. His reaction at the first sign of rising trout would dispel any doubts as to whether he is there for fishing or not. There is still a good measure of the animal in him. He must now yield to the poetry of the quest or blaspheme his sport.

See him circling the current, lengthening his line with deliberation and care. What became of the piety? Is this homespun mystic a fraud, after all? No. He is simply the multifaceted individual that most men are.

Underneath the day-to-day consistencies of labor and business there is a subcutaneous life of inherited multiplicity, a life which occasionally erupts and gets written about in the newspapers. The myth of singularity is one of the most unfounded of our common beliefs. If I appear to be inconsistent to another I rejoice in my normalcy. Some of it can be ascribed to fly fishing which is so inconsistent. But really, what is so damning about inconsistency? Isn't it time that we put aside the old bromide of consistency as an indicator of superior character? The criminal who is consistent gives us little hope for a better world; and only too often, consistency is a euphemism for dullness and lack of imagination.

Beginning with trout onward to Man, the histories of many species are replete with inconsistencies. But for those inconsistencies, I believe evolution would have been considerably hampered. Indeed, in certain species consistency may account for their imperviousness to change. In accepting these premises we acknowledge one of the most important lessons to be learnt from angling, and which, when applied to day-to-day experience, makes the unpleasantries less shocking than normal deviations with which we are prepared to cope.

The meaning of fly fishing may differ somewhat in each angler according to his history and personality. It may undergo some changes over the years, but seldom in its dynamic. If anything, it becomes intensified with experience, inclining him toward obduracy and even contentiousness. This is why I prefer to let others talk about the angling "fraternity." I will not say that the term is nonsense. I do not wish to offend. Let me say, rather, that it is romanticism or wistful thinking to assume that fly fishing is a catalyst for a particular democratic process. I do not find it so. As to my earlier reference to the streamside as a neutral ground, no democracy was inferred. Neutrality implies a truce among conflicting points of view. True, you may be able to get fly fishers together on an issue, say, capital punishment for netters, snatchers, and even bait fishers, but you'll have them together just long enough to satisfy themselves that the guillotine is working properly. If they join occasionally in organizations such as *Trout Unlimited* and other clubby societies it is because in the off-season they are the closest thing to a riverbank. Alone, virtually every fly fisher of experience is in that area of his being an outright individualist. In his public life he may be a joiner, a Rotarian, or a chamber of commerce bore; but at the river, with rod, line, and flies, he is transformed.

When an angler enters that precinct of his soul reserved for fly fishing he becomes aware of his uniqueness. The task allotted to him in society may be as inferior and mean as clerk in a department store, perched on one of the lower rungs of the economic ladder. Now, let us invite his boss, president, and Top Dog to the same streamside, and at once it will be evident that here indeed is God at his inscrutable best. The clerk will probably show some outward sign of recognition such as remembering the boss's name. He may even exchange a pleasantry with him or a fly. But unless the erstwhile Mister Big is something of a fly fisher, he must accede to the fact that here, alas, is his peer or, as likely, his superior.

Would a sea crossing contradict this? I doubt it. The landed English gentleman, owner of three miles of choice water, may be his riverkeeper's or ghillie's employer, and his ghillie will dutifully net the gentleman's trout. But the arrangement is a mutual convenience to which they tacitly consent. And when the gentleman has returned to his manor house, the real lords of the river take over. Their lives are inextricably bound to the river, and in exchange for their devotion to its maintenance, the off-stream gentleman will wisely write off his employees' peccadilloes to "research."

Should it appear that I have wandered, let me make one of those flash modulations, as in modern music: Fly fishers are not a democracy. They are as individual as the kings of ancient Ireland, which is said to have had more kings than counties or their equivalents. And now, without laboring the point any further, let me invoke the image of the true fly fisher who, whatever his social condition, at the waterside becomes exclusive owner of his soul, seeing its riches unfold before him, possessing on his own terms that which none other may appropriate: his own particular awareness of the mood of the morning stream. He is the lord of the castle and lands that are himself and his perception of the elements of his sport. How a nearby branch in full leaf bends over the water, it bends only for him, for that is his moment and place in Time and no one else's.

Devastating neuroses among fly fishers are virtually unknown. Obsessions, yes; but happily so, leading to the smug pronunciamento: "He is crazy for fishing!" But in our case the obsession is an integrating force which repels extraneous manic thoughts and sensations which could otherwise assail the personality with an effect as crippling as plucking the wings from houseflies. As for the lay person in trouble, the most successful and time-proven remedy is to go fishing—not necessarily fly fishing, but any kind of fishing. Medical men of every discipline who go fishing know this. But I doubt whether the psychotherapist will prescribe it. It just might be bad for business. And if it were applied in the universal sense, few of the fishermen and women among the entrenched and bastioned religions of the world would differ greatly on the importance of individual contentment to world peace and order. Fishing is the supreme distraction from the contrived and imagined differences in Mankind.

Rivers are best known to those creatures who live in or near them. If it were possible to communicate with them we should be reminded about many things which our species has long forgotten, or which exist in barely discernible feelings and attitudes, mere traces suggesting a more than imaginary influence from our heritage. Perhaps even this is an overstatement. Our involvements in the pursuit of careers or of earning livelihoods in a frenetic society do not encourage reflection, nor meditation profound enough to probe the depths of our feelings.

In our search into the secret life of rivers we could turn to the freshwater biologist. But the biologist, confined to the scientific method, could not extrapolate from his results the elusive thing we are looking for, namely, the spirit of the stream. This is the proper work of poets and other persons with readier intuitions than the scientist, and who are drawn to the river on less empirical quests, responding to their call not with collecting paraphernalia but with highly receptive sensibilities. Such men must be intensely human, by which I mean that each of them must be as aware of his presence and participation in an animal world as of his stature in it. He must be aware also—perhaps equally so—of its heritage. Only then can we ascribe to him a ready access to his intuition and instincts. This implies a certain multiplicity of personalities or beings; but it is this multiplicity, if one may call it such, which makes it possible for such men to communicate to us those insights which conjure up the sensations of an earlier time and of previous forms of life. The intimation of traces remaining from previous existences can give added depth and richness to our perceptions of ourselves, awakening us to a greater understanding of, and sympathy with, the lesser creatures and our fellow humans.

In considering the matter of Man's multiple personalities—and I think it is one of the few admissible concepts which can throw light on his inexplicable behavior—we must hark back to his evolutionary stages. It may help explain the why of an angler.

What is it, really, that brings the pleasure of anticipation in his preparations, the excitement on his way to the stream, and later the quiet exhilaration in watching the dimpling rise of trout taking insects at or near the surface? Is he identifying with the fish? He may, to some degree. But I am inclined to think that he relates to something farther up on the evolutionary scale. Speculating on where that might be, images appear and dissolve, leaving a well-defined form in sharp focus. It is that of an otter, whose head-form paused midway between that of a fish and man, a highly intelligent face suggesting a developed brain.

But more arresting perhaps is the otter's attitude. Anyone who has observed otters at home will concede an evolved sense of play in them which is carried over into the pursuit of their prey.

Every angler, I'm sure, carries some memories of halcyon days astream. But farther back in the dim recesses of his unconscious are the halcyon days of his predecessor; and I believe that his angling experience as a man, with its attendant joys are a dim and somewhat refined reverberation from his past. This, of course, can only be ascribed to the angler who is "in tune" with his dim past in a particular wave-line or unseen "wire" that is still carrying signals, however dimly, from the past. He is only too willing to play the flunky to his residual memory.

The angler scrambling down the streambank holding on to saplings with one hand, the other gingerly steering his favorite rod away from tangles, presents a different picture from that of a string of otters clambering up then sliding down the family mudbank. There is the chance, of course, of an unhappy coincidence should the angler slip and fall into the water with gashed waders and fractured rod. But given a satisfactory approach to the stream, as the hills raise their silhouettes over the setting sun, a unanimity of mood steals over both the angler and the otter. The latter's encroaching hunger has transferred his sense of play to a reach similar to that upon which the angler's eyes are focused, at the tail of a long riffle. There, among the tiny dimplings of emerging insects the wave-rings of rising trout have begun to flounce in widening circles. Biding their time a while longer, man and beast are waiting for that moment when the trout are darting and swerving into the main body of the hatch and caution is at a low ebb. The otter now slips into the water; a fly line begins lengthening . . .

The otter may kill more than he needs. He often does. It may be that the play motive has carried him beyond the bounds of necessity. The angler does not need the trout for sustaining his life. Is he then a killer for sport? Yes; but the kill is incidental to his sense of play in the sport. Cruel? No one knows for sure. But if so, far less cruel than bullfighting, house cats, usury, bad violin students, and the vendettas of divorce.

I have known the passion to stalk and play a trout to net with the singlemindedness of a hunting cheetah. I have then known days when I was content to saunter along the streamside merely to watch, to listen, to feel, to drink in with my very pores all that a summer day and Nature could bring to a waking sensibility. I have tied flies by the score, have invented some, and have participated in discussions on patterns and the differences in modes of dressing them. I have sifted the comparative merits of feathers, animal furs and hairs and their synthetic substitutes. I have attended exhibits of rare fowl with motives barely contained by admiration and restraint and have studied the possibilities in wild birds and ducks with an eye less Audubonian than calculating. I have read extensively, borrowing books from public and private libraries, and have purchased one or another when it was possible. I have gobbled up every book on English and American angling that was promising in one way or another. My purchasing record, however, is marred by one incident:

I was engaged one year to play with the Pittsburgh Symphony Orchestra. The little family took off in the old car, leaving the crisp, clean air of Catskill autumn for a city whose ugliness and grime soon cast a pall of gloom and depression on a life barely redeemable by music.

One day I wandered into a large bookstore. A title on the bookshelves of the used book department took my eye. I had never seen nor heard of the book. It was *A Modern Dry Fly Code* by Vincent Marinaro. Riffling through its pages, I began pecking at bits and pieces of a clear, lucid prose that shone with an originality that set it apart from other books on American fly fishing I had read. There was a hint of heresy about it that so piqued my curiosity that I was taken by an irresistible compulsion to purchase it. But how? I was broke. The first symphony checks had long been spent. My head began churning. Wedging the book between upper arm and ribs, I purchased a cheap paperback novel with the loose change I had left and later slipped the *Code* alongside the novel in its paper sack and walked out of the store almost sick with agitation—a most unlikely thief. It was the first and last book I ever stole.

Many years later, at an anglers' banquet in an upstate New York city, someone introduced me to the guest of honor, Vincent Marinaro. As he shook my hand his finely chiseled features softened.

"At last," he said, smiling. "I have kept your letter religiously. Do you remember it?"

"Yes, Vincent, I remember it, though not verbatim. It must be over twenty years ago."

"I'll never forget your prophecy that the book would reemerge one day, and successfully. It took me out of a profound depression. As you may know, the book had been remaindered. Your prediction gave me hope for its future. I don't know how to thank you."

I confess to having enjoyed a little glow of pride in having been vindicated by Marinaro's success. His *Code* had indeed reemerged at a time when fly fishers were better prepared to accept new ideas. The first edition had appeared too soon. As I had suspected then, fly fishers would be dubious about accepting the results of Marinaro's experiments with terrestrials, regarding them as violations of the established canons of traditional dry-fly design. Much of the success of the second edition was owing to the vision of its editor, Nick Lyons, who shared my conviction that it was a classic of American fly-fishing literature and subsequently published it.

I am reasonably certain that, in this rather personal and subjective review of fly fishing, certain thoughts may appear odd, whimsical, perhaps even bizarre; but such is the nature of my private affair in the world of angling; accordingly, I have nothing to contribute which might add to the sum total of angling knowledge. I do not care to learn all there is to know about fly fishing beyond that which fulfills my particular need. Simply, there is not enough time to learn all there is to know. I prefer, rather, to pursue the sport on my own terms, going about it in accordance with my own true nature, for when I have deviated for one reason or another, I found myself losing the poetry of it. The lines were then false, distorted. But it may be precisely because of my backslidings that I saw the desirability of being freed of them. It was only when I had come to accept myself that I realized angling had become one of my roads to personal liberty—one of the greatest of life's gifts.

Knowledge of the many aspects of fly fishing is valuable only insofar as it can add dimension to one's personal enjoyment of the sport. This will be better understood by those anglers who have come round to the deep conviction that the catching of many fish or of great fish is no guarantee of fulfillment in the sport. The measure of true success then, is the quality of one's fishing determined more or less by the ways in which the angler's sensibilities have responded to and communed with his surroundings, the mood of the day and of the water. When these are attuned together, the action need only be minimal to complete the chord of fulfillment.

In our time of dwindling resources it seems ironic that warped values are being so widely disseminated toward the catching of more fish. If we could reverse these values instead toward the conservation, protection, and careful regulation of what we have left, there would be a decided lessening of the pressure for greater yields of fish. Instead, the sporting media—principally the popular sporting magazines and how-to-catch-more-fish books—all seem bent on exterminating the trout from our remaining waters. Had their extermination been planned maliciously it could scarcely have improved upon the efforts of big and little businesses to sell more and more tackle and equipment. And selling, we must all know, is sacred to us. It all seems like a nightmarish conspiracy. As long as Nature is at the mercy of Business we can be sure of leaving to our children the legacy of a handful of dead houseflies.

In these pages I have used the word "men" perhaps too often. I hope that when it could apply, the use of the plural has been read by women in the inclusive sense. An important event in the history of angling not only justifies the inclusion but actually mandates it to a degree that may prove unsettling to condescending male anglers of the manly sort, and somewhat bewildering to those who assume that our angling literature begins with Izaak Walton.

To the best of our present-day knowledge, the first person to have written a book on angling in the English language pre-dates Walton by some 200 years and its author is a woman. She was Dame Juliana Berners, prioress of the nunnery at Sopwell, England. Her book, *A Treatise of Fishing with an Angle,* is a truly astonishing work which covers the subject in remarkable detail with an endearing clarity of prose beginning with the superior merits of angling over other country sports. She gives clear instructions for preparing baits for differing fish, describes and illustrates varying rigs for bottom fishing, how to make one's own hooks, rods, and lines and, happily for the modern fly fisher, gives the dressings for artificial flies for every month of the fly-fishing season!

Dame Juliana's was not only the first book on angling, but, as in other firsts in the history of civilization, it became the model for angling books in the centuries to follow.

After having done with her explicit directions for tackle, and methods of angling for each particular fish, Dame Juliana sets forth a code of angling behavior which could well be a model for the modern angler. The following is quoted from *The Origins of Angling* by John McDonald (The Lyons Press):

> I charge you that you break no man's hedges in going about your sports, nor open any man's gates without shutting them again. Also, you must not use this aforesaid artful sport for your covetousness, merely for the increasing or saving of your money, but mainly for your enjoyment and to procure the health of your body, and more especially of your soul. For when you intend to go to your amusements in fishing, you will not want many persons with you, who might hinder you in your pastime. And then you can serve God devoutly by earnestly saying your customary prayers. And in so doing you will eschew and avoid many vices, such as idleness, which is the principal cause inciting a man to many other vices, as is right well known. Also, you must not be too greedy in catching your said game (fish) as in taking too much at one time. . . . That could easily be the occasion of destroying your own sport and other men's also. When you have a sufficient mess you should covet no more at that time. Also, you should busy yourself to nourish the game in everything that you can . . . And all of those that do in accordance to this rule will have the blessings of God and Saint Peter . . .

Dear Juliana, no one writing on the pleasures of a country sport was ever provided with a more fitting finale than your code of sportsmanship, for whose use I am immensely grateful. In acknowledging your admonitions as implicit prayer, perhaps you will permit me to append an "Amen" for our time, as you would have had you been born 500 years later to share our dismay:

—And I urge you to protect your waters from the ravages of greedy and ruthless men, however powerful they may be, and from their debaucheries of them by pollution, mindless deviations, and other desecrations; for afterwards there may be no streams, only dismal channels for pestilential flows and loathsome sludges, and our spirits may never be raised again by the beauty, purity, and laughter of flowing waters.

FAREWELL TO FLY FISHING

I HAVE WRITTEN elsewhere on some aspects of fly fishing, dropping a confession here and there, or what seemed to me to be a revelation. While holding to the truth—that is, mine, I had not been as generous as I could have been in embracing a more inclusive—or, dare I say it?—the whole truth, in my having barely averted a catastrophic turn of fate in the sport. A brief history of this event may prove instructive, if not totally acceptable to other anglers. I refer to the memorable year of my farewell to fly fishing.

How this unlikely premise could have had its beginnings has touched some anglers, usually the married ones, and those matrimonially inclined but living in sin.

It began in the last week of September in, if I remember, the mid-seventies when the sound of a distant bell began tolling the knell of the dying season.

This is the time of year when an uneasiness mounting over the last weeks culminates in a sorrowful view of falling leaves floating aimlessly in slow circles around eddies, resuming their drift to settle in their final resting places at the bottom of some distant reach downstream. Anglers are not misled by the implied gaiety in the bobbling colors, knowing it to be a visual swan-song reverberating inwardly as a dirge for the angling year.

On the homeward drive, thoughts of having to put the rods away began their dismal counterpoint to the surging tune of the car as the drooping leaves of the Catskill forest shone wanly in the lingering twilight.

I recalled my feelings on having to turn away from the river bank. An ominous sense of finality had pervaded them. Was this to be my last look at the river? For some time I'd been having sneaky misgivings over the wayward life I'd been leading. A slumbering Puritan had begun stirring awake.

At home my wife greeted me affectionately. I returned Marlene's kiss in a somewhat dutiful lackluster way. She had sensed the gravity with which I had taken the rod carrier to the den. She asked anxiously:

"Did something go wrong, dear? Was the fishing dull? I can't imagine it. You always say there is no bad fishing, only good and better. What could have happened?"

"Nothing much," I said listlessly. She knew I was equivocating, but did not protest, knowing the solemnity to be a preoccupation with some unknown matter.

In the ensuing days the Puritan, now fully awake, had begun making his rounds with a dour tenacity vaguely remembered from some near-forgotten times when, following upon some resolve, I had decided to mend my ways, as when I'd curbed my thirst for Irish whiskey, and again when I'd stopped smoking Italian stogies, to Marlene's relief and gratitude. I'd had mixed emotions about it, for those acrid little ropes were staunch repellents against the waterside mosquitoes and vicious black flies. Which was why we seldom saw houseflies indoors. They just died.

But this time it was fly fishing itself which was sitting with me on the judicial dock.

Puritan began his preliminary examination and subsequent accusations. He had appeared before on certain occasions when I'd managed to dismiss him for the sake of my peace of mind; but this time the curmudgeon had caught me in a weak moment: It had been one of the worst seasons I'd ever known. He was snapping away, his blue nose sharp as an accusing finger:

"Does the defendant have any good reason to have shirked his duties every week for the sake of tormenting innocent fish?"

I said I was not quite sure, but had no desire to torment trout; only to catch them and then release them.

"Do you mean to sit there and tell me you released them all?"

"Well, no. I kept one now and then."

"Indeed you did! I remember the ones you creeled, poor things. However, to your credit you did dispatch them mercifully. How many have you strangled?"

"I don't remember exactly; but not many."

"Why all that strangling?"

"Well, I felt I should take one home to my wife. She loves to eat trout. If I didn't take one home occasionally she'd wonder why I fly fished at all."

"That's very well, but did this so-called sport justify the loss of weekend after weekend, and then a two-week vacation with those fishing-bum pals of yours, the loss of income—man, on what grounds can you justify those expenditures, those rods? How many do you have now?"

"Only seven."

"Only! Split cane, of course!"

"I wouldn't use the synthetics."

"Other anglers do, and are pleased with them."

"They don't know any better."

"They don't, eh? And what did that Payne cost you? The Halstead, the one by Walt Carpenter. Peanuts?"

"No. Not exactly. You see, each is superb in its own particular way, on one stream or another under varying conditions."

"Very specialized, eh? I call it self-indulgence. Do you remember what you paid for just the Payne and the Halstead? Don't answer that question. You'd lie, as you have to your wife. Let me tell you! Twelve hundred dollars! And what about those capes you bought last spring? Three more blue duns and what others, do you remember?"

"Well, the grizzly was one of the best I'd ever seen. The straw ginger was irresistible."

Puritan's lips thinned to a taut narrow line, his nose had got sharper, verging on purple.

"And that on top of all the material in that twenty-four–drawer cabinet of yours, the metal boxes of flank feathers: wood-duck, mallard, teal, bronze mallard, the tools, the extra vise, the silks, the hooks, hooks, hooks; thousands of them. Shame! Can you guess at the amount you've frittered away?"

"Yes, it's quite a bit; but remember, I've been collecting over twenty-five years, so it doesn't amount to that much every year. Besides, the variation in color among the capes is important for making flies according to variations in patterns and the insects themselves. One fly takes the dark dun, another the rusty dun, still another the medium, and so on—all necessary—"

"You fly tyers are disgusting—all for the sake of tormenting the poor fish—"

"It's a grand sport, sir."

"Grand? Sport? You lie through your teeth! It's a vice! An ungodly vice."

As Puritan's accusations went burrowing into my conscience I felt the proddings, then the shovings of remorse. I remembered Marlene once having to choose a less expensive dress. She would have looked beautiful in the other. This was right after I'd bought the eight-foot Payne, the same year my violin and viola students had fallen away to fifteen. Could Puritan have been right in calling me a monster of depravity?

As winter drew on I took the rod carrier out of the den, carried it upstairs to the attic and carefully stood it up in the darkest corner. As I descended I lowered the trap door with a dubious mix of conviction and virtuousness in having overcome some nagging flaw of character and began stepping about the house with a renewed sense of purpose.

December arrived with furious blasts of chilled winds that assailed the groaning pines. The long, grey days followed one after the other, relieved from time to time by brilliant sunlight that lent a glittering patina of purity to the already pristine snow. The weeks fell away imperceptibly as I attended to the growing skill of my students in the afternoons and evenings. Mornings I spent shaping a long memorial essay on a dear, late friend who, as a violin-maker, had become a reincarnation of one of the great masters of the Golden Period of Cremona. A man of genius, he had restored the lost art, tonally and visually, bringing joy to players for whom the older master instruments had become financially prohibitive. I had undertaken the task of making the greatness of a modern maker credible in our time and of invalidating the objections of antiquarians, players and dealers both. As the words formed on paper, a reach of the Beaverkill River would appear between the lines like the tantalizing glance of a beautiful woman beckoning then fading as I scribbled away.

Past years, when the January blizzards had relented, the warming trend would find me hovering over the fly-tying desk in my den, setting my fiddle fingers to making one fly or another. But this year the impulse was dormant. I sensed the change that had come. Significantly, the Beaverkill woman had not reappeared and I began to look with renewed interest at Marlene as she went about her tasks with cheerful grace. I saw then how really beautiful she was. I told her so, congratulating myself on my good fortune. I think she had sensed the change taking place. One day she took me close and said, wryly, "Frank, you still haven't tied a fly. Usually, by now you would have tied quite a few."

"Darling," I replied, "things are a bit different." I said no more, not wishing to elaborate on my resolve.

Then, unexpectedly, Marlene fell ill. This loyal, loving angel had never given me cause to regret my courtship and a life together that had been gratifying despite certain idiosyncrasies and backslidings of mine which she had tolerated with more than a trace of maternal concern.

Her illness was all the more alarming, since for weeks it had defied any medical diagnosis. She had become weak, listless. The pallor that overspread her face, arms, hands, and her lovely lips had prompted a forced cheerfulness on my part as I padded about the bedroom attending her as best I could. Thoughts of a possible loss and its shattering consequences were followed by moods of profound melancholy.

By degrees, the thought that I did not deserve her was growing to conviction. How many weekends and prolonged holidays had I left her at home to her solitary readings, the radio, the television, or to an occasional female friend? True, I had tried to make it up to her in certain ways with a gift of flowers or a dinner out, away from the stove. These, and other gestures, had been rather feeble attempts to atone for my omissions. And now I was seeing the ominous shadow of retribution that was crouching nearby.

To suppress this image I wandered into my den, pulled open the top drawer of the big chest and saw the reels. With the exception of some spare spools all but four were by the great House of Hardy. Handsome, functional, with satisfying, purring clicks, the various models represented a trove of which the most fastidious angler would be proud: Featherweights, LRH's, Princesses, Perfects, Zeniths—I had gloated over them all in the past; but now my guilt was taking me by the throat. A sudden impulse overpowered every thought. That evening I rang Roger.

"Roger," I said, "would you try to sell my rods for me?"

There was silence, then Roger burst forth, loudly.

"Frank, have you gone out of your mind?"

"I don't think so," I replied, continuing evasively. "Simply, Marlene is sick. We're going to need the money." Had I told Roger the truth, that I had decided to say good-bye to fly fishing, he would not have believed it, or would have suspected me of having got religion, excoriating me for being such an ass.

The next day I brought the rod carrier down from the attic and left the entire battery at Roger's, leaving him dumb with incredulity.

Marlene began to recover, imperceptibly at first, then with convincing vigor. There came the day when, well on her feet, she cooked the first dinner in six weeks.

Not long after, I rang Roger.

"Rog, how many rods did you sell?"

"None," said Roger. "I put the word out, but no one showed any real interest."

"You're lying, you bastard!"

"No, I'm not!" he snapped. "When I told them whose rods they were, they refused to believe me. One even called me a liar, as you did!" A few days later, the rods were back.

During Marlene's illness my resolve had become a hardened fixation. At times I would be aware of talking to myself in a way that made my decision irrevocable. While a core of gloom underlay my day-to-day life I would rouse myself to a lighter mood, muttering cheerful thoughts and congratulations on revealing an unsuspected store of character, after all. I began to anticipate the looks of disbelief passing among my pals when they learned that the impossible had happened. I imagined the chorus: Whatever happened to Frank, the fly fisher par excellence? It reminded me of the time I asked a native Catskillian about a woodcutter we had known who passed away.

"Wal," said he, "Alex quit drinkin', he quit smoking, he started goin' t' church, an he up an died." I thought sadly on poor Alex. It had been, literally, an appalling price to pay for his reformation. This thought, juxtaposed against my resolve, began questioning the virtues of reformation, then burrowed downward into some unknown niche to work its devious ways.

In quiet moments of reflection I would call to mind some of the angling pals who had accompanied me on one jaunt or another. All good men, each in his own way, but somehow flawed. To one degree or another, each had become addicted to the sport, and as I recalled their habits, compulsions, and idiosyncrasies I began to feel an old kinship and camaraderie slipping away, replaced by a melange of compassion and pity. Poor devils! Hopelessly mired in the treacherous bog of fly fishing! They needed help, these old friends, but didn't know it. And should they have known it, would have had no inclination to suspend the habit, say less of breaking it. They were the unregenerates who would resume flogging the waters at the first breath of spring.

I remembered Big Del, whom we had dubbed "The Scourge of the Delaware." Unsurpassed as a caster, his meticulous Marinaro patterns had bilked many large, strong trout from the river to which his soul had got so attuned. One evening at his home his lovely wife wryly confided her narrow escape from spinsterhood on the occasion of their civil marriage. They were about to enter the courthouse when Del stopped abruptly, his arm and brow glued to a telephone pole. Alarmed, Diane stood by anxiously, asking whether he was ill. Del blurted his inability to go on with the marriage. Seemingly unmoved by her winsome beauty, he made no move to enter the magistrate's office until he had extorted her promise that she would never interfere with his fishing (and hunting) weekends save for an occasional holiday with her, and later, the family. She had wept in gratitude and joy for this magnanimous concession, admiring him all the more for his manly honesty. In such manner are born anglers put on earth to assert their prerogatives in the sport. Intending better, the Lord's hand does nonetheless falter and, whether by design or whimsy, makes a very crooked line indeed!

Such behavior is not uncommon in the brotherhood. It is really too bad because some of our maladroits are otherwise good and even decent men. Again, it is really unfortunate, for, sooner or later, the vice gets out of hand. As it did for me one July day on the Beaverkill when, at dusk, as darkness had nearly obliterated the pool and I was about to quit I hooked, played, and landed a brown trout that weighed a scant five pounds! We took it in triumph to the Antrim Lodge and lay it in state on the bar of "Keener's Pool," the basement bar and restaurant.

Various anglers crowded round, toasting the fish, the captor, and buying drinks for the house. One wag, who was obviously not in pain, announced that he had studied for the priesthood and that such a noble fish deserved to have a Requiem Mass sung over him. Hearing him botching the sequences I assumed, hazily, that he had probably been thrown out of the seminary. As he intoned the *Dies Irae* I saw a furtive tear here and there, probably from old altar boys, except for Joe Rabinowitz, who had been moved to lachrymose solemnity by the spell of the alcoholic ritual.

Fortunately for me, Roger, who had stayed with beer, insisted on driving home, for which I was grateful. It was five o'clock the next morning when he deposited me at my door. A pallid Marlene was waiting, tears of relief in her reddened eyes. How I was put to bed remains a vague, shameful memory. The fish proved uninviting, smelling of stale slime, beer, and alcohol.

Continuing the roll-call, I arrived at the irascible Ron, who was a good enough stream companion, but who, offstream, would show an impatience rising to choleric fits of disapproval of pompous or arrogant non-anglers, "ignorant pigs," as he called them, adding some back-alley epithets that were scarcely flattering. I learned that Ron had exhausted what little patience he had with women. His wife had had an unfortunate tendency to nag. One morning she was at it again, accusing him of not being helpful about the house like other husbands. Ron flung the plate of scrambled eggs at her and took off with his tackle. He never came back. As he explained it later in his mobile home, he could dispense with the amenities of marriage but not his fishing.

Such were the men whom I'd admired and whose stream manners had been models of courtesy and consideration. But at what, or whose cost? Some had, perhaps inadvertently, come close to becoming Jekyll and Hyde personalities: impeccable gentlemen astream; elsewhere, ruthless, shiftless impostors who spent their daily lives feathering their weekend and holiday nests. Were these the gentle anglers of literary tradition? Or were they really monsters of deception? In one way or another, each was a skillful, self-centered fraud. Even Roger, whom I had regarded as a consummate angler, and whom I had held in near-awe as a modern reembodiment of Theodore Gordon, was blissfully unaware of having no place or purpose in Society. In his ignorance he probably thought it was the name for an anglers' club on the banks of some unknown river.

There was another member of our company of anglers whom I nearly overlooked, not imagining why; for in his quiet, unobtrusive way, Bill was the subtlest among the serpents concealed in the bankside tangles of the sport.

Good old Bill had retired after some years of a job emptying the coffers of a huge city hospital's store of coin-operated TV sets and was resting from his Herculean labors by fishing the Catskill and Adirondack streams, some of which were probably unknown to the Geologic Survey. Bill knew every stream and river in the state, and had at one time or another fished them all. Unmarried, he went his unfettered ways, the envy of all the anglers who had been domesticated. Good-natured, amiable, the best of river companions, he too, like Roger, had a sublime disregard for the entanglements of Society, in whose eyes he was regarded as the prince of fishing bums. Having done his stint in the Army's Pacific island campaign, he had washed his hands of all lethal weapons, substituting for them the rod that seemed to be an extension of his hand.

Thoughts of Bill and my other angling amigos recalled the plaque I had once seen in some tavern or other: "Allah," it said, "doth not deduct from man's allotted years the time spent in fishing." Whoever it was that authored this pronunciamento had had a prophetic but incomplete inspiration. A quick calculation indicated the time my cronies had spent in anticipation, preparation, and fishing itself had taken virtually no toll. I estimated their average ages at about eleven and a half years.

One morning I wandered over to my bookshelves and saw the many angling books I had amassed over the years. Some were rare, others had become scarce; and for these I'd handsomely laced various dealers' wallets. If my library was not extensive enough to have pleased an angling scholar or collector, it was comprehensive and varied enough to provide a sound foundation of angling lore in points of entomology and artificial patterns of flies, the life and character of differing rivers, their tributaries, methods of angling for the differing species of fish under varying conditions, a historical survey of the sport, the evolution of equipment, books on the art of fly tying, memoirs, sketches, essays, and stories, singly and in anthologies. These were but a small part of the literature that the sport had spawned, numerically far greater than for any other sport. Many of the "greats" were there, the poets and philosophers, such as Haig-Brown, Lampman, Fedden, Lyons; then the noted entomologists and anglers, Ronalds, Halford,

Skues, Sawyer, Wetzel, Jennings, Marinaro, Flick, and Saint Theodore Gordon of the early American years.

The British had spent considerable portions of their lives conniving against the strangleholds of wealth and privilege on the fishing rights to chalkstreams by forming clubs for doling out short reaches or "beats" to members, like crumbs to starving birds, that each might have a taste of the sport of princes for a few hours. It all seemed somehow pathetic. In America Theodore Gordon had endured savage winters in a garret in Sullivan County, warming his hands over the feeble fire of a small stove, that he might tie flies for a small clientele, keeping body and soul together. That men would make such sacrifices poses the question, "Why?" At this point in my life it all seemed incomprehensible.

I saw Izaak Walton peeping from a shelf and pulled his *Compleat Angler* out. I turned to his "Milkmaid's Song," reading it again: "Come live with me and be my love / And we shall all the pleasures prove." All the pleasures, no less! The horny old bastard! I'd heard far more learned men than myself waxing sentimental and even reverent over this book, and I wondered why such a fuss had been made over those feeble imitations of the old Latin writers. I discerned at last why this pious fraud's book had gone through scores of editions over the centuries, reaffirming the truth that, by and large, mediocre men are attracted to the writings of their own kind, thus giving a sound rationale for Walton's enduring success. Having said this, I felt a great load had lifted from my conscience, the ensuing easement compatible with my resolve to free myself from an old bondage.

As the bitter flails of February sent the days scurrying toward March I began to look up at the trap door to the attic where the rods had been resettled together, reiterating the vow to mend my way by severing old compulsions toward a new-found freedom. Ah-h!—liberation, at last! I began to consider whether the rods should be brought down, after all, that they might thaw gradually, so as to be in perfect condition for a possible sale to other anglers still struggling ineffectually within the meshes of the vice.

Marlene saw me coming down from the attic one morning with the rod carrier, a puzzled expression on her face. I informed her, "I'm getting them ready to sell. The season isn't far off. They'll be looking for rods." She seemed wistful, but I wasn't quite sure.

A week or so into March, the phone rang. I heard Roger's voice. It was jaunty, cheerful. He had evidently thawed out. "Frank!" he bellowed, "Do you know that it's only a couple of weeks to Opening Day?" He was, as usual, exaggerating. It was precisely three weeks and three days. To make conversation and not offend this good but weak-minded man I replied, "Well, Rog, March is taking its time about it, isn't it? Are you getting ready? Tied any flies?"

"Frank, I must have tied ten dozen at least!—started New Year's Day to celebrate getting over the hump. How about you?"

"Well, I came close to tying one on the other night, but it wasn't a fly." I felt something getting out of hand. I was getting chummy again with this good but corrupt man.

"Hey, Frank!" he bawled on. "We haven't had much snow! The run-off isn't going to be much. The stream shouldn't be too high. Maybe like last year. Remember? Quill Gordons! Dry! On opening day! God, wasn't that something? Hadn't happened in maybe twelve years! We had a mind-blowing day, remember? It just might be a replay of last year."

"Roger!" I said, sternly, "I'm still going to sell my rods!"

I heard a choking sound, then an explosion of breath. "Frank! Have you gone batty? You've some of the most perfect casting instruments I've ever laid hands on. The Payne is a masterpiece!" An image of that gentle genius, James Payne, flitted through my mind. That dedicated master! I was about to sell him down the river! There was a catch in my throat. A crevice was cracking open. I was getting uneasy. "Rog," I said, hoarsely, "I left something on the stove. Excuse me."

I had left nothing on the stove; but Marlene had. Dinner was in the making. I wandered from room to room then went out the door to look at our rhododendron bush. The frost-wilt had gone out of its leaves. They were green and smooth again. Spring had been sneaking in again on slippered feet. The sun had begun setting and its path had veered toward the vernal equinox. I heard a cheerful feminine voice. "Dinner is about ready, dear!" I re-entered the house.

"Darling," I said. "Forgive me, but I think I'll pass. But I'll join you at the table." I poured a soft white wine for her and a Martini for myself. We sipped in silence. Later, as she nibbled at her food I poured myself another. In the evening a student came in for her weekly lesson. I was grateful when she left. It had been very trying. She seemed to have regressed. I bid Marlene good night and retired to one of the side-by-side twin beds. As I sank into a deep sleep, an ominous dream began shaping.

Under the lurid sky of a strange city some young men and teen-aged boys were running aimlessly about the sterile streets. Two were brandishing handguns and soon began shooting at random. But no victims fell. As the bullets struck, the intended victims clapped hands on parts of their bodies and laughed hysterically. The bullets were probably of cork or some other harmless substance. Then they saw me and began to screech, "Let's take care of this bastard!" They ran around a corner. Suspecting some mischief, I hurtled round and stopped abruptly. My rod carrier was lying limp on the sidewalk. The rods had been taken out of their cases and were heaped together. Nearby stood my fly-tying cabinet. Two of the boys upended the drawers and formed a pile. I recognized the blue dun capes, the light ginger, the reds, the light browns, and grizzlies. Heaped next to the capes were the fur pieces, the teal feathers, the precious wood-duck flank feathers, and a scattering of sundry other materials. One of the boys lighted a match and a curl of smoke began rising. Then I saw smoke rising from the pyramid of gleaming bamboo: There was the Payne, the Carpenter, the Winston, the Halstead, the Edwards Quadrate, the Orvis. I ran forward and began kicking at the flames. In a rage I began to shout and scream, pummeling one after another of the vandals. They were laughing uproariously. One of them had got his arms around me. I was fighting him off when I heard an agitated feminine voice: "Frank! Frank! Wake up!" The horror dissolved. I sat up in bed. The light was on. Marlene was holding me, murmuring, "Frank, dear, you've had a bad dream!" I cast off the sheet and quilt, perspiring. An hour later I went to sleep again, safely ensconced in Marlene's comforting arms. For the moment I had regressed to a child again, and I did not protest.

In the morning I narrated the dream to Marlene. She was strangely silent, except for a murmur of sympathy.

The shock of the dream remained with me in a less vivid and terrifying form. Underneath the frequent recalls, a faint message, at first undecipherable, began taking a less apocryphal character, edging a bit closer to making sense yet never revealing anything in tangible form. From what had remained of the dream I'd begun to suspect that I had somehow escaped a dreadful fate. I began opening the rod carrier almost daily, unscrewing the brass caps of the aluminum cases, joining one then another of the rod sections and flexing rods. I visited the den frequently, always opening the drawers where the blue dun capes lay, identifying each one and recounting them to be sure.

During the last week of March the phone seemed to have shaken off its winter torpor and began to ring daily, at times late at night. Angling conferees from whom I hadn't heard for months were on the move again. The Rip van Winkles of the angling world seemed to have wakened at once and were looking toward the friends of their long pre-sleep.

While fragments of that dreadful dream still lingered, its message was burrowing deeply with growing intensity, but I held fast to my resolve that I should free myself from the habit.

However, a moroseness had settled inwardly, making any sort of civil response difficult, even irritating. I heard myself snapping at unprepared students, and even Marlene was not spared.

On the last day of March the phone rang. I picked up the receiver and recognized Roger's voice instantly. "Hey, Frank!" he shouted. "The day of deliverance is at hand! The frost is only skin deep, and the forecast is for warmth, sun, and some cloud!" He continued, "Judd called and said he saw a Quill Gordon take off! Just imagine if there should really be a hatch! How about meeting me at Winchell's Corners at eleven? On the stream by twelve-thirty, and be all ready if the hatch should come out!" I began wavering, sensing something, a membrane perhaps, cracking and parting inside.

"Rog," I said, not wishing to hurt his feelings—a very sensitive man, Roger, a prince of a fellow, goodhearted, loyal—I heard myself saying, "I'll just go along to look at the river." I hung up. My hands were trembling. Marlene had been listening. She looked up, smiling. "Old Gloomy," she said, "Crusty! Had you been trying to—well—what? Reform?"

That night sleep refused to come. An hour or so before dawn I slept restlessly, then came fully awake and made coffee. Shortly Marlene awakened and took the cup I had prepared for her. She sipped it slowly, got up and made breakfast. Afterward I began to look for my fishing vest. It was not in its usual place. Nor my tackle bag. Nor my waders. Nor my rods. A feeling of panic began surging up with a residue of my dream terror. Marlene saw me emerge from the den, saw the empty hands twitching aimlessly.

"It's all in the car," she said. "Locked," she added, smiling.

"I packed everything yesterday afternoon. Now I'll make lunch for you and Roger."

At about three o'clock that afternoon I took my first trout of the year, a lively, spunky female. As I unhooked her I kissed her on the nose. I'd almost swear she kissed me back. As she swam away, I laughed for the first time in how many weeks? I could not remember. But I was myself again, unrepentant, whole and free.

As for my tormentor, he never accosted me again. I think he left for the Happy Hunting Ground of Puritans.

THE MAYFLIES

FROM TIME TO TIME these melancholy days, as I cling to the remnants of a life sliding into oblivion, I think on Pierre Van Ruysdael, the eccentric, half-mad Dutch violin virtuoso with whom I'd chosen to study during the mid-years following on early manhood.

His career as concert violinist had been brought to an abrupt end by a disastrous marriage and he had accepted a professorship at a northern New York university. When he heard my audition he offered me a full scholarship, welcoming the advent of a young man who had already been a member of a respectable symphony orchestra and who held promise of rounding out toward the higher reaches of violin playing, already showing glimpses of a richening artistry. The teacher-student relationship soon acquired the added dimension of a friendship with occasional invitations to dine with him and his new wife, for which I was grateful; but for a handful of private students I should have had no income at all.

Pierre found in me an eager and most willing assistant, capable of relieving him of the burden of teaching the less talented and somewhat indifferent students. In time, a shared passion for fly fishing for trout led to occasional flights to regional streams in his car at speeds more suggestive of the Grand Prix European races in which he had competed than of casual investigations of reportedly promising waters. These trips, undertaken in a fury of anticipation, would find us far from a designated stream, ending at some unknown waterside with the predictable results of empty creels, which did not deter us from making exploratory trips to other streams, for we were pursuing the eternal chimeras of the classic fly fisher.

Pierre had been one of the most promising of a brilliant coterie of violin students of the great Belgian master, Ysaye, and had also studied orchestral conducting with Nikisch, the foremost conductor of his time. Accordingly, when the directorate of the regional symphony orchestra came available, he leapt into the post and shortly proved his ability to infuse the group with renewed energy, providing a leadership of persuasive musicality of a high order. Concerts under his direction drew enthusiastic reviews from the media critics, fetching audiences and admirers from considerable distances. Pierre and his wife, Sophie, soon found themselves increasingly sought-after by the social luminaries of the region.

One day Pierre proposed that I accompany him on a visit to a small city, to which he had been invited by Robert McKinnon, a prominent industrialist, and his attractive young wife. Pierre was especially pleased by the prospect of fishing a private stream owned by McKinnon's fellow executive.

On our arrival, a robust man skirting the mid-sixties greeted us affably in a solid, spacious, well-appointed house with extensive grounds. It was mid-morning, and the coffee was still hot. We sat at a large oak table as McKinnon poured coffee. He pointed to the cage of the house elevator. "Lyris is on her way," he said. "She'll soon be down." Shortly we saw the descending elevator. As it stopped, the elevator gate opened. A lovely young woman stepped out, kissed Pierre and acknowledged Pierre's introduction of his young guest with a warm, hospitable smile.

"Your name," she said, "sounds Italian. Am I correct?"

"Yes," I said, "Italian on both sides."

She went to a sideboard and returned with some luncheon dishes. As unobtrusively as possible, I noted the gracefulness of her hands, the pellucid fairness of her arms and throat, the soft, madonna-like oval of her face highlighted by lustrous blue eyes and crowned by an undulating cascade of shoulder-length blonde hair. The conformation of her breasts barely restrained an encroaching plumpness accentuated by her short stature. Probably in her early thirties, she was an exotic bloom at the peak of fullness gracing this American barony.

Suppressing any overt show of the overwhelming pleasure I was taking, I joined Pierre and McKinnon, who were speculating on the merits of the trout stream to which McKinnon had secured permission for us to fish that afternoon. "I'm told," he said, "there are mostly brown trout. The brookies are in the upper stretches."

I marveled at the disparity in ages of this grossly mismatched pair. He was easily old enough to be her father. His grey hair, verging on white, seemed to have spilled over on his face. Lyris interposed, asking Pierre about his wife.

"Sophie iss fine," he said. "She wass unable to join us. She sends her love."

"Please give her mine," said Lyris, "and be sure to tell her I'm planning to come and see her soon." At this I felt a surge in my rib cage at the thought of seeing this exquisite creature again at my friends' house, well away from her affluent and superannuated custodian.

McKinnon gave Pierre directions to the stream, and as we prepared to leave, he took off for his office at the plant. As Pierre went to our car, I thanked Lyris and accompanied her to the elevator.

"I hope you will stop by again," she said with a touch of shyness, adding, "I was in Italy for some years. In fact, that's where I met Mac. Do you speak Italian?"

"To a limited degree," I said, "some of it in dialects. But I manage fairly well at times. Let me say I feel privileged to have met you. *Sono incantato.*"

At this confession of enchantment she flushed bewitchingly and recovering, replied, also in Italian, "Your *gentilezza* brings much pleasure. *Grazie.*"

Reluctant to leave, I lingered, held by wonder and a mysterious, encompassing force. She opened the elevator gate and I hung there a moment. "I'd never before seen a feminine angel," I said. "The privilege is beyond explanation or description."

A shyness had crept again into her smile. She replied, again in Italian, so appropriate to the lilt of her voice. "You are very kind. I am so pleased at having met you."

"May I look forward to your visit to Sophie?" I asked.

"Of course!" she replied. "I shall try in a week or two at most. And I, too, will look forward to seeing you again. Sophie will know." She began closing the gate. *"Arrivederci,"* she said as the elevator rose out of sight.

Images of Lyris and the reverberations of our parting words accompanied every cast I made that afternoon as the stream prattled away in sunlight and shadow. The trout were coming to my flies with the eagerness and abandon that mark the halcyon day. Downstream I could see Pierre's rod springing in an occasional arc. The perfection of the afternoon seemed to have been made in celebration of a new and wonderful event. A vague image of fulfillment was preying about the rhythms of the looping line, and the mayflies struggling to take wing were my own departures from a prosaic existence in which I was now learning at first hand the meaning of the word "transformation," for I was in love, and the promise of a multidimensional life of transcendent beauty had begun to unroll prophetically with the flowing current.

A few evenings later, at dinner with the Van Ruysdaels, Sophie said Lyris had phoned. I stopped chewing and hung over the table, charged with expectancy. Sophie went on. "She'll be coming by next week." She turned to me directly. "She asked about you. She seemed more than merely curious—quite different from her charmingly casual self. She seemed eager to know all that I knew of you. What did you do to her?" Sophie's reserve had softened into a wry, mischievous smile.

"Nothing, really," I said. "You might ask, rather, what did she do to me!"

"What?" she asked.

"Everything," I replied. "Simply, I was overwhelmed by her beauty, her graciousness. Since then I've not been able to suppress a desire to see her again. It all seems like an impossible dream."

"Dream?" Sophie smiled. "It seems to be heading for something more substantial than that, and quite real. Lyris will be driving her Italian housekeeper to visit some relatives downstate. She asked me to invite you to go along with them. It may be a bit rash in view of Mac's constant vigilance. He's very possessive and obsessively jealous of any attentions from men, especially young men. He married her when she was very young, probably as young as his daughter by an earlier marriage, whose mother died when the child was in her teens."

"Thank you," I said, "but I can't find it in me to refuse her invitation. Should either of you ring each other, please tell Lyris I shall be honored to accompany her."

My week passed feverishly. Practicing seemed futile, the days a succession of garbled images of her loveliness and of the threatening incubus of her old husband. On the appointed day Lyris turned into the Van Ruysdael driveway in a large, sleek Cadillac. Sophie led her and her aging maid into the living room where I was waiting, suppressing a rising agitation as well as I could.

Lyris came forward, extending her hand. I took it tenderly, raised it to my lips and kissed it, looking into her eyes with the adoration overflowing from within. As the pink flooded her face she murmured, "*Grazie.* I'd like to introduce an important member of my family, Signora Beatrice Taddeo."

Beatrice extended her hand with the unadorned grace that characterizes the mature Italian woman of domestic service.

Lyris addressed her in Italian. "Beatrice, this is my friend, the violinist, Franco Beltrami." Beatrice smiled and nodded, acknowledging the young man her mistress had invited to share the drive.

"Lyris," I said, "I'll be happy to drive, if you so wish."

"Thank you," she said. "It's more than kind of you to be our chauffeur, a luxury both Beatrice and I would enjoy."

Our destination was about two hours away over improved roads into the southernmost reaches of the Onondaga Reservation where brooks with Indian names flowed, and where Pierre and I had fished.

We deposited Beatrice at her brother's house with the understanding that we would return to fetch her after her visit.

As we retraced our route, the roadside shadows had lengthened, and dusk was approaching. I saw a small wooden bridge ahead which spanned a stream. "Lyris," I said, slowing down, "let us go look at the water." I pulled the car over to the side of the road, opened her door and assisted her. She took my arm and we crossed the road to the bridge. We stood at the railing, arm in arm. The stream had darkened except for patches of broken water which reflected the paling sky. Below us, a trout rose. As the surface rings flounced, I saw other rises breaking the surface at various points. Insects were hovering over the stream, and I knew a hatch of mayflies was in progress. I turned toward my beautiful companion.

"Lyris," I said, "those little rings are part of the recurring metamorphosis of the insect life of this stream. They are taking wing now, and many will not escape the trout. But those that are lucky will fly off to the trees for a night or so, shedding their skins and emerging with new bodies and transparent wings. We call them spinners. They will converge at various points above the stream and begin their nuptial dance. They will have lost all desire for nourishment, having come round to their ultimate purpose, driven only by love and the instinct for perpetuation. Later, exhausted, they will fall, one by one with wings spent. Their eggs will slowly sink into the depths to lie in the crannies and silt to await the time of emergence next summer to another cycle of life."

"Franco," she murmured, "the story is tragic, but everlastingly beautiful."

We turned to each other and our hands reengaged, twining about each other. I met her upturned face and our mouths merged. I led her across the bridge. We turned into some shrubbery and found a glade where the consummation of our love lay waiting for the release that came with a surge of joy. Later, in the pale light of a rising moon we took flight again, searching and finding ourselves high above the waters of our universe. Hand in hand we crossed the little bridge to the car and drove off in a silence that was thundering in my ears, Lyris seated close as we drove off, wordless, sunk in awe of the contract which had been sealed.

As we sat together in Sophie's driveway, aware of the necessity of having to observe discretion in the eyes of Lyris's hostess, we spoke of our love, and whether it could prevail against the strictures of her marital condition and her very possessive and jealous husband.

"I will ring Sophie when I can," she said. "She is a dear and sympathetic friend who understands our situation, and will gladly relay my messages."

"Lyris," I replied, "I can't imagine being away from you for long. I love you utterly and completely."

"I know," she said. "And I love you as if I'd been reborn to it. I shall miss you awfully, deeply, and will find some way of coping with this depressing stranglehold of being exclusively Mac's property."

The parting kiss lingered a long, painful moment. She went into the house and I took off in my old Ford roadster, a noisy and unpredictable third-hand affair which I did not yet own.

The ensuing days dragged on interminably, alternating between indifferent practice sessions, lessons to private students in my shabby, one-room apartment, orchestra rehearsals, and one or another of Pierre's students. Daydreams wove in and out of the dreary days, images of a lasting, redemptive love, of marriage and of beautiful children from that divine creature. There were recurring mementos of that idyllic consummation of our love and the indelible celebration of our epiphany in a stream-bank bower. There was then an insistent hope that nature's triumph had wakened to life an embryo that even now had begun its voyage to the light of a future day, loosing the bonds of a wretched marriage.

Later in the week as I was preparing for a student at Pierre's college studio room, the phone rang. Sophie's voice sounded in the receiver. Her usual slow, measured delivery had shifted to a lighter key, a blend of gladness and urgency. Lyris had phoned saying she was coming to town on the coming Monday at early afternoon, adding, "Please tell Franco to be at your house."

Despite the wearisome intervening days, Monday did manage to struggle through. I appeared at Pierre and Sophie's at midday. Luncheon dishes had appeared and I was cordially invited to join them. I declined with thanks. Whatever appetite I may have had had got elbowed aside. I went outside and stood in the driveway in a furor of expectancy. When the big Cadillac turned into the driveway, I stood by to open her door. She stepped out with a radiant smile. As I took her in my arms, I saw a big, black car in the street. It was going by very slowly.

Lyris went inside to greet Sophie and Pierre, and emerged shortly. "I would like to go for a drive in the country," she said.

"Dear one," I replied, "nothing would please me more. Would you deign to go with me in my little puddle-jumper?"

"I'd love to!" she cried, gaily. I led her to my little roadster and she got in. "How charming!" she said as I sat at the wheel. "This is ever so much more a fun car than mine."

As I turned the key I addressed the car. "Old Ford," I said solemnly, "be mindful of whom you have the privilege of carrying. No shenanigans, please! Be on your best behavior. You have never been so honored!" She gave a low, delicious laugh as she snuggled close.

We drove out of the city, past the green drumlins and the wide expanse of the country club's golf course. As we entered the open country the cars began thinning out in both directions. A few that were following soon passed us. One did not.

Frequent glances into my rearview mirror showed the big, black car maintaining its pace at the same distance. An uneasy thought crept into the silence. I recalled the large black car cruising slowly by the Van Ruysdael residence earlier and now marked the similarity to the car that was dawdling behind us. Could it be a coincidence?

I turned off into a dirt road which crossed some outlying farms, and as I turned into another lane I looked into the rearview mirror. The black car had turned into the lower road and was slowly crawling our way.

Farther up our lane I had seen a grove of mostly deciduous trees which held some promise of a bucolic haven somewhere within. I slowed, looked back and saw the black car had stopped. Its meaning had become purposed and ominous.

I turned to Lyris. "Darling, we're being followed."

Lyris turned to look out the window. "Where?"

"There," I pointed. "See that line of trees where the farm lane turns up off the main road?"

Her reply sounded as from afar. Her voice had sagged. She looked again and I saw her tremble slightly. "Good old Mac," she said, nodding slowly in disbelief.

"Has this happened before?" I asked.

Her lovely head swung quizzically. "I don't know for sure," she said, "but somehow he has known where I've been, and with whom. I've often wondered how he knew so much."

I swung my thumb up and backward. "That's how," I said. "Detectives. Hired agents; flunkies of the well-to-do captains of industry."

I pushed the car onward, hoping to regain the highway by the next farm road leading to it. The black car followed at a considerable distance. As we turned toward the city we took our place in traffic and eventually arrived at the Van Ruysdael house, still bound by the seething silence of the pursuit. As we stood in the driveway, the black car crawled past in the street. Two men were seated side by side in it. As they passed, the driver's companion turned to look at us fixedly, in final verification, I supposed, of our identities for their report on Lyris's venture with her young man.

Days went by, sinking into the slough of weeks. Now and then, the oppression that bore down with Lyris's absence and total silence was relieved by a dinner with Pierre and Sophie. Though invariably warm and hospitable, my friends had totally avoided any comment on Lyris's silence, sensing the quiet gnawing of an unutterable loss. Our topics were mostly music and fishing.

As the summer wore on, a letter arrived from the manager of the Central City Philharmonic Orchestra. Would I care to return? The conductor had asked him to inquire. He had learned of my progress under Pierre's tutelage and of some solo appearances of mine which had drawn praise. He was prepared to offer me a position as one of three alternating concert-masters. The concert season had lengthened. The minimum wage had been increased, and that of leading positions proportionately so. A teaching position was opening up at the conservatory. Would I accept it?

I told Pierre and Sophie about the offer. Both urged me to accept, and I did so with regrets, for a warm bond of friendship had grown among us during my years there. At a farewell dinner they finally broke the hiatus of any reference to Lyris.

"Franco," Sophie began, "we have reason to suspect Lyris was placed under house arrest. She cannot make a move without Mac's consent. We've learned from the grapevine that they seldom entertain anymore, and the few friends they keep are carefully screened. Mac's daughter is the exception. She is quite close to them; one might say, fatally so. There is something you should know."

At this Pierre broke in with a blasphemy in the mangled English which had barely survived the Dutch, French, and German influences of his European studies. It came in an abrasive bass: "It iss un goddamt shame!" In his lean, lupine face his blue eyes were glittering angrily. "It wass terrible to do vot he did to a lofely, innocent woman! Sophie you tell Franco how it wass!"

Sophie paused a moment. I was picking at my plate. She resumed slowly, in a voice which had modulated to an undulating drone: "Mac had been married to the mother of this grown daughter of his. The girl had barely entered her teens when the mother began showing symptoms of a disease which was then little known to the medical profession. It drew her down dreadfully, and in time it became evident that she was wasting away. Sensing the inevitable, the future security of her child had become her foremost concern. Medical efforts had proven unavailing. One day she called Mac to her bedside and swore him to the promise that, should he remarry, he would never sire another child. Moved by pity, Mac agreed to abide by her dying wish.

The foregoing and the remainder of Sophie's monologue sank like ingots into an inner crucible, melting, cooling then hardening to impervious memory. Save for a few personal digressions, I retained her narrative as if it had been engraved in stone. I transpose it nearly verbatim:

Some time after his wife's death, Mac went to Italy on company business. In an enclave of Rome he met a family of American emigres who had lived there in a modest villa for many years. Their only daughter was the beautiful and charming Lyris, then just turned twenty-two and much sought-after socially in both Italian and American circles, especially by adoring young males.

Mac was so struck by the young woman's beauty and charm that he resolved to win her despite the wide disparity in ages. An astute businessman, he had learned of the financial straits in which Lyris's parents had got bogged down, and with typical American pragmatism made them an offer which would liquidate their debts and ensure their future ability to live as expatriates in Rome.

Lyris and her parents had been very close. A bond of love and mutual respect had grown stronger over the years, and when she got wind of the precarious state her parents were in, she yielded to Mac's offer of marriage.

Reconciled to her new life in the States, Lyris was informed one day of Mac's vow to his dying former wife and submitted to the hysterectomy which would forever deprive her of her feminine birthright. Mistress now of all the amenities provided by a successful and affluent husband, Lyris did not become fully aware of her great loss until love came into her life. As the implications dawned on her, she began to feel the impact of the outrage which had been perpetrated upon her. I remembered Sophie's final words as if they were at once a curse and a prophecy of an unendurable, soulless deprivation ahead. Pierre was nodding sorrowfully. "He wass un monster!"

The few mouthfuls I had taken were only half-chewed and had stuck in my throat. A vague but compelling image of Lyris confined to her baronial quarters drifted about in my fogged brain. Later, I turned to Sophie, "She never called?"

"No," she said. "I wouldn't put it past him to have threatened to harm you. She would never have risked the possibility of it on the man she loved, and probably always will."

I left early, embracing both in turn, and we parted in silence.

I returned to the Central City Philharmonic Orchestra. As season followed season, I began to hear the creakings of encroaching age in myself as I'd already heard it in the Van Ruysdaels in our holiday calls. The gaping voids recurring after my return had become less frequent, leaving only fragments of lessened pain as the immediacies of my marriage took on greater meaning with the advents of a son and daughter. Their growth and developments owed much to the love and intelligence of their mother, a choice which was never to be regretted.

I had often harked back to my studies with Pierre, our fishing trips and the many kindnesses of the Van Ruysdaels. Often, too, I wished I could have thanked them adequately. Then, in an inspired moment, I named my son Pierre. My friends were pleased and moved, for they had no children of their own.

During my seven-year absence from the Central City Philharmonic, many changes had taken place. Those lingering traces of amateurishness had been replaced by a very high standard of competence. The string, woodwind, and brass choirs were now equal to the demands of the ever-growing complexities of the literature. Our conductor also happened to be one of the leading concert pianists of his day, a genial but exacting Spaniard whom the entire orchestra was capable of accompanying with faultless precision in major concertos at home, on tour, and in recordings. At the Conservatory, a new generation of violin students was reflecting the escalating national standard of performance then in progress.

Each spring I would feel the inner wakings to the call of the stream, a spring creek which nourished an old trout hatchery an hour's drive south, and which gave access to the lower, unprotected reaches. But its insect life had required modifications in tactics, for its mayflies had been supplanted by a proliferation of the hardier caddisflies. However disquieting this was to my ideal, it was better than no fly fishing at all.

Eventually, young Pierre's interest in fly fishing became so compelling that he became my partner, a full-fledged and competent fly fisher.

Thirty years had gone by. One Christmas Day, Sophie and Pierre rang. Both sounded quite tired. Had Sophie ever heard again from or about Lyris? Yes. Mac had died some years back, leaving her quite comfortable, financially; but not physically, for she had had to pay the price of the distressing consequences of her old hysterectomy. She had become obese, fleeing friends and retreating in shame from the onslaughts upon her former beauty. She had gone back to Italy and was living in her parents' villa, a recluse.

Another six years passed. One fall day the phone rang. It was Sophie, telling me Pierre had passed away in sleep. Later, Sophie entered a rest home for the aged.

The uncertainty of the years remaining does not dismay me. The pension is adequate, and the children are making their way as promising adults.

In a clause of my Last Will and Testament, I have specified that upon my death my ashes are to be strewn into a riffle on the East Branch of the Delaware River, as I did Pierre's with Sophie at my side, into a stream we had both loved on the Onondaga Indian Reservation. If my son and daughter carry out this last wish faithfully, my ashes will surge downstream in a milky veil to settle by degrees among the rocks, crannies, and silt of the watercourse whose banks I once walked in a benison of pure contentment.

Aware now that only the rite remains, shorn of any ultimate purpose, it must prevail, if only as a ceremonial tribute to the source of life itself.

There, of a summer evening, the mayfly nymphs will start drifting by, crawling out of their shells to flutter upward and away. And high above the river, last night's spinners will begin their nuptial dance. Lyris will be among them, suspended, her wings a brilliant blur. I shall rise out of the ashes to join her and we shall go spiraling off on an ancient, timeless quest.

But no eggs will fall. For reasons better known to mankind than to mayflies, her right to perpetuity had been snatched away.

Later, she will fall to the water, exhausted, her wings spent and still, to disappear round a bend in the river. Now is the flash of a trout below, followed by a gaping mouth, a descent into a watery vortex and the long night of a viscous dissolution.

We shall not reappear, save in faint, fleeting remnants of dreams of a blameless love consecrated in innocence and joy, transcending the trials of lives mortal, fragile, and flawed.

As ours were. As are those of mayflies and men. And will ever be.

ENVOI

The music for *An Angler's Anthem* first appeared in a song by Franz Schubert, "The Trout." The tune was later incorporated as a theme with variations in Schubert's celebrated *Trout Quintet* for piano and strings.

This version was first sung in 1976 at a celebration of the landmark legislative victory by the citizens' group, *Catskill Waters,* over the City of New York, putting an end to the capricious, often disastrous, releases from city reservoirs into the rivers resulting in periodic fish kills over many years. The law transferred the custodianship of the releases to the New York State Department of Environmental Conservation, which maintains a just regulation of flows.

FRANK MELE
1911–1996

I first met this little man with the pipe and big voice one late-April day along the banks of the East Branch of the Delaware River. It was Hendrickson time in the Catskills and we exchanged pleasantries as we waited for the first duns to emerge. If my memory is correct, the flies never appeared and we soon went our separate ways. I recall that he wore a Greek fisherman's cap and held a cane fly rod that he said was a Payne. Little did I realize on that blustery spring day some twenty-five years ago that our paths would cross again in the effort to restore several of the Catskills' most important trout rivers.

In 1973 Frank formed Catskill Waters, a coalition of local anglers dedicated to increasing the flow of water from several New York City reservoirs. His efforts resulted in the Water Release Legislation of 1975, a law that required the city to restore and stabilize flows in Esopus Creek and the East and West branches of the Delaware. Many people feel that this was one of the most important fisheries-related conservation victories of the 1970s, and it would not have occurred without Frank's leadership and tenacity.

Frank lived most of his adult life in Woodstock, New York. He was an accomplished violinist and teacher of the violin and the viola; and he was a totally dedicated fly fisher. In 1973 he wrote "Blue Dun," a story in this volume that explored the mystique of natural blue-dun hackle; it first appeared in

149

Fisherman's Bounty, a collection of stories, poems, and essays edited by Nick Lyons. Nick also published Frank's novel about an immigrant Italian in Rochester, New York, *Polpetto,* in 1973, which received high praise from Christopher Lehmann-Haupt in the *New York Times.* A first version of *Small in the Eye of a River* was published in 1988; three additional essays, written in the last years of Frank's life, have been added to the current edition.

Frank died on November 16, 1996. A group of friends sprinkled his ashes over the riffles of his beloved East Branch, at Shinopple, on April 6, 1997.

—TONY BONAVIST

Hurley, N.Y., 1998